I0438955

Mercury in Indiana Watersheds: Retrospective for 2001–2006

By Martin R. Risch, Nancy T. Baker, Kathleen K. Fowler, Amanda L. Egler, and David C. Lampe

Prepared in cooperation with the Indiana Department of Environmental Management

U.S. Geological Survey Professional Paper 1780

U.S. Department of the Interior
U.S. Geological Survey

U.S. Department of the Interior
KEN SALAZAR, Secretary

U.S. Geological Survey
Marcia K. McNutt, Director

U.S. Geological Survey, Reston, Virginia: 2010

For more information on the USGS—the Federal source for science about the Earth, its natural and living resources, natural hazards, and the environment, visit http://www.usgs.gov or call 1–888–ASK–USGS.

For an overview of USGS information products, including maps, imagery, and publications, visit http://www.usgs.gov/pubprod

To order this and other USGS information products, visit http://store.usgs.gov

Suggested citation:
Risch, M.R., Baker, N.T., Fowler, K.K., Egler, A.L., and Lampe, D.C., 2010, Mercury in Indiana watersheds: Retrospective for 2001–2006: U.S. Geological Survey Professional Paper 1780, 66 p. plus appendixes.

Preface

If you are reading this report, you probably have a reason to learn more about mercury in Indiana watersheds. Your reason may be linked to your involvement with fishing, outdoor recreation, science, and resource management or to concerns about one or more of Indiana's watersheds. This preface addresses those reasons to make the report relevant to you.

If you are like many Indiana adults, you enjoy catching and perhaps eating fish from Indiana streams and lakes. You may have some questions about the fish you catch and that you and your family eat. One question may be about mercury—a colorless, flavorless metal that is known to be present in a very small amount in many fish. If you consult one of the annual Indiana Fish Consumption Advisory booklets or check online, you will learn that mercury cannot be removed from the fish by cutting it out or cooking it out. Health officials in Indiana have advised that some sizes and species of fish or fish from certain streams or lakes should be eaten infrequently or not at all because of the potential health risks associated with mercury in the fish. They state that these health risks are greatest for young children, the unborn, and new or expectant mothers, who may be advised to avoid some fish from Indiana streams altogether because of mercury.

Most Indiana adults participate in outdoor recreation (92 percent, according to a recent survey). If you enjoy boating, hiking, bird watching, nature study, hunting, or other outdoor pursuits, your experiences are enriched by the wildlife. You may not know that mercury can negatively affect the reproduction and early development of wild birds and mammals, but this problem has been documented by scientists. Mercury accumulates in the food chain in aquatic ecosystems so that creatures at the top of the food chain acquire the highest amount. Mercury also accumulates in forest canopies, but the mercury exposure in food chains of forest ecosystems has received less study than those of aquatic systems.

If you are interested in the quality of the environment, you may know some of the issues involving mercury. If you work in natural-resources management, environmental protection, or earth science, you may deal with mercury issues. Knowledge gathered by studies of mercury in natural systems worldwide during the past 20 years has provided a scientific basis for concern about effects on humans, fish, and wildlife. Findings have indicated that human activity has a dominant role in releasing mercury into the environment—into the air and the water. Experimental evidence indicates that it is the mercury most recently introduced to water, often from the air, which primarily enters the food chain.

Groups of scientists have proposed a national plan to monitor the indicators of change in ecosystem responses to mercury contamination. The plan emphasizes the value of integrated, long-term monitoring for documenting progress in reducing mercury in the environment on a large scale, such as a state, a region, or a nation.

For a statewide scale, monitoring data have been collected over a time span long enough to present a retrospective view about mercury in Indiana watersheds. Watersheds are the land areas that drain surface water. Watersheds make meaningful boundaries for grouping and interpreting mercury monitoring data and information about landscape characteristics, human activities, and natural communities. The purpose of this report is to summarize and interpret the occurrence of mercury in Indiana watersheds for the decade preceding 2006, primarily for 2001–2006. Changes in the levels and distribution of mercury that result from regulatory actions and pollution-prevention initiatives after 2006 can be compared to this baseline. Public officials and interested citizens can evaluate policies and programs directed toward mercury with the perspective of the data and interpretations in this study.

—M.R.R.

Contents

Figures

Tables

Appendix 1 Tables

Conversion Factors

Multiply	By	To obtain
micrometer (µm)	0.00004	inch (in.)
centimeter (cm)	.3937	inch (in.)
meter (m)	3.281	foot (ft)
kilometer (km)	.6214	mile (mi)
mile (mi)	1.609	kilometer (km)
square meter (m^2)	10.76	square foot (ft^2)
square kilometer (km^2)	.3861	square mile (mi^2)
square mile (mi^2)	2.590	square kilometer (km^2)
cubic meter (m^3)	35.31	cubic foot (ft^3)
gram (g)	.03527	ounce, avoirdupois (oz)
kg (kilogram)	2.205	pound, avoirdupois (lb)
million gallons per day (Mgal/d)	.04381	cubic meter per second (m^3/s)
cubic feet per second (ft^3/s)	.02832	cubic meter per second (m^3/s)

Temperature in degrees Celsius (°C) may be converted to degrees Fahrenheit (°F) as follows: °F=(1.8×°C)+32

Horizontal coordinate information is referenced to the North American Datum of 1983 (NAD 83).

Concentrations of chemical constituents in water are given in nanograms per liter (ng/L). Concentrations of chemical constituents in solids are given in milligrams per kilogram (mg/kg) and micrograms per kilogram (µg/kg); 1 mg/kg is equivalent to 1,000 µg/kg.

Concentrations of mercury in air are given in picograms per cubic meter (pg/m^3).

> A kilogram is 1,000 grams.
> A milligram is 0.001 gram, and 1,000 milligrams equal 1 gram.
> A microgram is 0.001 milligram, and 1,000 micrograms equal 1 milligram.
> A nanogram is 0.001 microgram, and 1,000 nanograms equal 1 microgram.
> A picogram is 0.001 nanogram, and 1,000 picograms equal 1 nanogram.

Atmospheric mercury deposition rates, atmospheric mercury loading rates, and stream mercury yields are given in micrograms per square meter per year (µg/m^2/yr).

Stream mercury loads from watersheds and atmospheric mercury loads to watersheds are given in grams per year (g/yr).

Turbidity is given in nephelometric turbidity ratio units (NTRU).

Abbreviations

GEM	Gaseous Elemental Mercury
GIS	Geographic Information System
IDEM	Indiana Department of Environmental Management
MDN	Mercury Deposition Network
NACWA	National Association of Clean Water Agencies
NADP	National Atmospheric Deposition Program
NLCD	National Land Cover Database
NWS	National Weather Service
PHg	Particulate-Bound Mercury
POTW	Publicly Owned Treatment Works
RAPIDS	Regional Air Pollutant Inventory Development System
RGM	Reactive Gaseous Mercury
USGS	U.S. Geological Survey

Acknowledgments

The authors are most grateful for the exceptional contribution of James Stahl, biologist with the Indiana Department of Environmental Management Office of Water Quality Surveys Section. James is the individual most responsible for the database of mercury concentrations in fish tissue used in this study. He provided the information in a highly organized format and supplied ideas for its interpretation

Mercury in Indiana Watersheds: Retrospective for 2001–2006

By Martin R. Risch, Nancy T. Baker, Kathleen K. Fowler, Amanda L. Egler, and David C. Lampe

Abstract

Information about total mercury and methylmercury concentrations in water samples and mercury concentrations in fish-tissue samples was summarized for 26 watersheds in Indiana that drain most of the land area of the State. Mercury levels were interpreted with information on streamflow, atmospheric mercury deposition, mercury emissions to the atmosphere, mercury in wastewater, and landscape characteristics.

Unfiltered total mercury concentrations in 411 water samples from streams in the 26 watersheds had a median of 2.32 nanograms per liter (ng/L) and a maximum of 28.2 ng/L. When these concentrations were compared to Indiana water-quality criteria for mercury, 5.4 percent exceeded the 12-ng/L chronic-aquatic criterion, 59 percent exceeded the 1.8-ng/L Great Lakes human-health criterion, and 72.5 percent exceeded the 1.3-ng/L Great Lakes wildlife criterion. Mercury concentrations in water were related to streamflow, and the highest mercury concentrations were associated with the highest streamflows. On average, 67 percent of total mercury in streams was in a particulate form, and particulate mercury concentrations were significantly lower downstream from dams than at monitoring stations not affected by dams.

Methylmercury is the organic fraction of total mercury and is the form of mercury that accumulates and magnifies in food chains. It is made from inorganic mercury by natural processes under specific conditions. Unfiltered methylmercury concentrations in 411 water samples had a median of 0.10 ng/L and a maximum of 0.66 ng/L. Methylmercury was a median 3.7 percent and maximum 64.8 percent of the total mercury in 252 samples for which methylmercury was reported. The percentages of methylmercury in water samples were significantly higher downstream from dams than at other monitoring stations. Nearly all of the total mercury detected in fish tissue was assumed to be methylmercury.

Fish-tissue samples from the 26 watersheds had wet-weight mercury concentrations that exceeded the 0.3 milligram per kilogram (mg/kg) U.S. Environmental Protection Agency (USEPA) methylmercury criterion in 12.4 percent of the 1,731 samples. The median wet-weight concentration in the fish-tissue samples was 0.13 mg/kg, and the maximum was 1.07 mg/kg. A coarse-scale analysis of all fish-tissue data in each watershed and a fine-scale analysis of data within 5 kilometers (km) of the downstream end of each watershed showed similar results overall. Mercury concentrations in fish-tissue samples were highest in the White River watershed in southern Indiana and the Fall Creek watershed in central Indiana. In fish-tissue samples within 5 km of the downstream end of a watershed, the USEPA methylmercury criterion was exceeded by 45 percent of mercury concentrations from the White River watershed and 40 percent of the mercury concentration from the Fall Creek watershed. A clear relation between mercury concentrations in fish-tissue samples and methylmercury concentrations in water was not observed in the data from watersheds in Indiana.

Average annual atmospheric mercury wet-deposition rates were mapped with data at 156 locations in Indiana and four surrounding states for 2001–2006. These maps revealed an area in southeastern Indiana with high mercury wet-deposition rates—from 15 to 19 micrograms per square meter per year ($\mu g/m^2/yr$). Annual atmospheric mercury dry-deposition rates were estimated with an inferential method by using concentrations of mercury species in air samples at three locations in Indiana. Mercury dry deposition-rates were 5.6 to 13.6 $\mu g/m^2/yr$ and were 0.49 to 1.4 times mercury wet-deposition rates.

Total mercury concentrations were detected in 96 percent of 402 samples of wastewater effluent from 50 publicly owned treatment works in the watersheds; the median concentration was 3.0 ng/L, and the maximum was 88 ng/L. When these concentrations were compared to Indiana water-quality criteria for mercury, 12 percent exceeded the 12-ng/L chronic-aquatic criterion, 68 percent exceeded the 1.8-ng/L Great Lakes human-health criterion, and 81 percent exceeded the 1.3-ng/L Great Lakes wildlife criterion.

Annual stream mercury yields were calculated with a model by using the mercury concentrations in water samples and daily average streamflows for 2002–2006, normalized to the watershed drainage areas. The average annual total mercury stream yields ranged from 0.73 to 45.2 $\mu g/m^2/yr$ and were highest in two White River watersheds in central Indiana. Median methylmercury stream yield was 1.9 percent of the median total mercury stream yield.

In most watersheds, average annual stream yields of total mercury were a fraction of the combined average annual atmospheric mercury wet-deposition and estimated annual dry-deposition loading rates, indicating that much of the stream mercury was attributable to atmospheric deposition. In two watersheds, average annual stream yields of total mercury were approximately twice the atmospheric mercury loading, indicating that some of the stream mercury apparently was not attributable to atmospheric deposition. Rather, some of the stream mercury yield potentially was contributed by mercury in wastewater discharges.

Land-cover type corresponded with the mercury levels in three watersheds: (1) A watershed of the White River in central Indiana with a high percentage of urban land cover had some of the highest total mercury concentrations and stream mercury yields. The urban land cover and numerous permitted wastewater outfalls with mercury in treated effluent potentially contributed mercury to this watershed. (2) A monitoring station on the Maumee River in northeastern Indiana, downstream from a large area of urban land cover, recorded the highest stream mercury concentrations. The urban land cover and mercury detected in treated effluent potentially contributed to the high mercury concentrations at this station. (3) A watershed of the Patoka River in southern Indiana with a high percentage of forest land cover had the highest atmospheric mercury dry-deposition rate. The high dry-deposition rate from the forest land cover potentially contributed to the high mercury concentrations in this watershed.

From a retrospective view, mercury concentrations in Indiana watersheds routinely exceeded criteria protective of humans and commonly exceeded criteria protective of wildlife. Atmospheric mercury wet deposition was a predominant factor, but not the single factor, affecting mercury in Indiana watersheds. Mercury in wastewater discharges and atmospheric mercury dry deposition apparently contributed a substantial part of the mercury yield from some watersheds. Dams and impoundments increased the percentage of methylmercury in downstream waters. Long-term monitoring of mercury in wet and dry atmospheric deposition, and in streams and reservoirs, coordinated with monitoring of mercury in fish, will be needed to detect whether mercury levels in Indiana watersheds change in the future.

Introduction

Mercury is a public-health concern and a threat to wildlife because it accumulates and magnifies in food chains. The State of Indiana has designated mercury as a "bioaccumulative chemical of concern" (Indiana Administrative Code, 2007a). Indiana watersheds constitute a valuable resource for water supply, recreation, and wildlife habitat. This report presents information about the geographic distribution of mercury in water and fish of Indiana watersheds for 2001–2006 and interprets factors that influence mercury concentrations and loads in water. During the analysis that resulted in this report, more than 384,000 data values were assembled and computed from mercury-monitoring records, mercury-source inventories, ancillary data, and maps of land-cover classes. This information was organized and examined for 26 watersheds that drain most of the land area in Indiana.

Mercury Cycling in Aquatic Ecosystems

Mercury is a metallic element that is found worldwide, arising from natural sources and dispersed through human activity. Mercury can be released by volcanic eruptions, forest fires, volatilization from oceans and continents, fossil-fuel combustion, waste incineration, and industrial processes (U.S. Environmental Protection Agency, 1997). Aquatic and terrestrial ecosystems receive mercury from wet and dry atmospheric deposition (U.S. Environmental Protection Agency, 1997; National Research Council, 2000), and this deposition occurs even in remote areas (Fitzgerald and others, 1998). In some places, discharges from stormwater-collection systems and from wastewater-treatment plants add mercury to aquatic ecosystems (National Association of Clean Water Agencies, 2000).

Inorganic mercury in ecosystems can be converted to organic methylmercury by micro-organisms as a byproduct of their metabolism. Methylmercury is highly absorbable, and the amounts in primary producers are preserved in successively higher levels of consumers in the food chain (Munthe and others, 2007). After atmospheric deposition or wastewater discharge contributes inorganic mercury to surface water (fig. 1), mercury enters a complex cycle in which one form can be converted to another, as explained by Krabbenhoft and Rickert (1995). Inorganic mercury in the water can enter sediments by particle settling and later can be released into the water by diffusion or resuspension. Mercury in the water can be released back to the atmosphere by volatilization and later can redeposit to water. Organic carbon relates to the levels and mobility of mercury in water, enhancing the availability to the food chain (Grigal, 2002; Brigham and others, 2009; Chasar and others, 2009). The way mercury enters the food chain is not fully understood and probably varies among ecosystems. Sulfate-reducing bacteria, which process organic matter using sulfate in the environment, take up inorganic mercury and convert it to methylmercury (Morel and others, 1998). The conversion of inorganic mercury to methylmercury is important because methylmercury is more toxic than inorganic mercury and organisms require a longer time to eliminate methylmercury. Methylmercury-containing bacteria may be consumed by the next higher level in the food chain, or the bacteria may release the methylmercury to the water, where it can adsorb to plankton and periphyton (Bell and Scudder, 2007). Plankton are consumed by the next level in the food chain (fig. 1). The concentration of methylmercury magnifies in organisms at higher levels in the food chain. Some methylmercury can convert back to inorganic mercury or enter sediments by way of particle settling. Details of the aquatic-mercury cycle are still areas of active research.

Total mercury and methylmercury in water have been monitored in many ecosystems and are expected to be an indicator of response to changes in atmospheric mercury deposition, according to Mason and others (2005), who state that interpreting the response of mercury concentrations in water to changes in atmospheric mercury input may be difficult.

Water concentrations can be influenced by factors unrelated to mercury inputs, such as variation in organic carbon and particulate matter. Studies have shown a correlation between atmospheric deposition of mercury and mercury in fish (Cocca, 2001) and between methylmercury in water and in fish that reflects changes at the base of the food chain, including a prediction that mercury-emissions reduction will rapidly decrease methylmercury concentrations in fish (Harris, Rudd, and others, 2007).

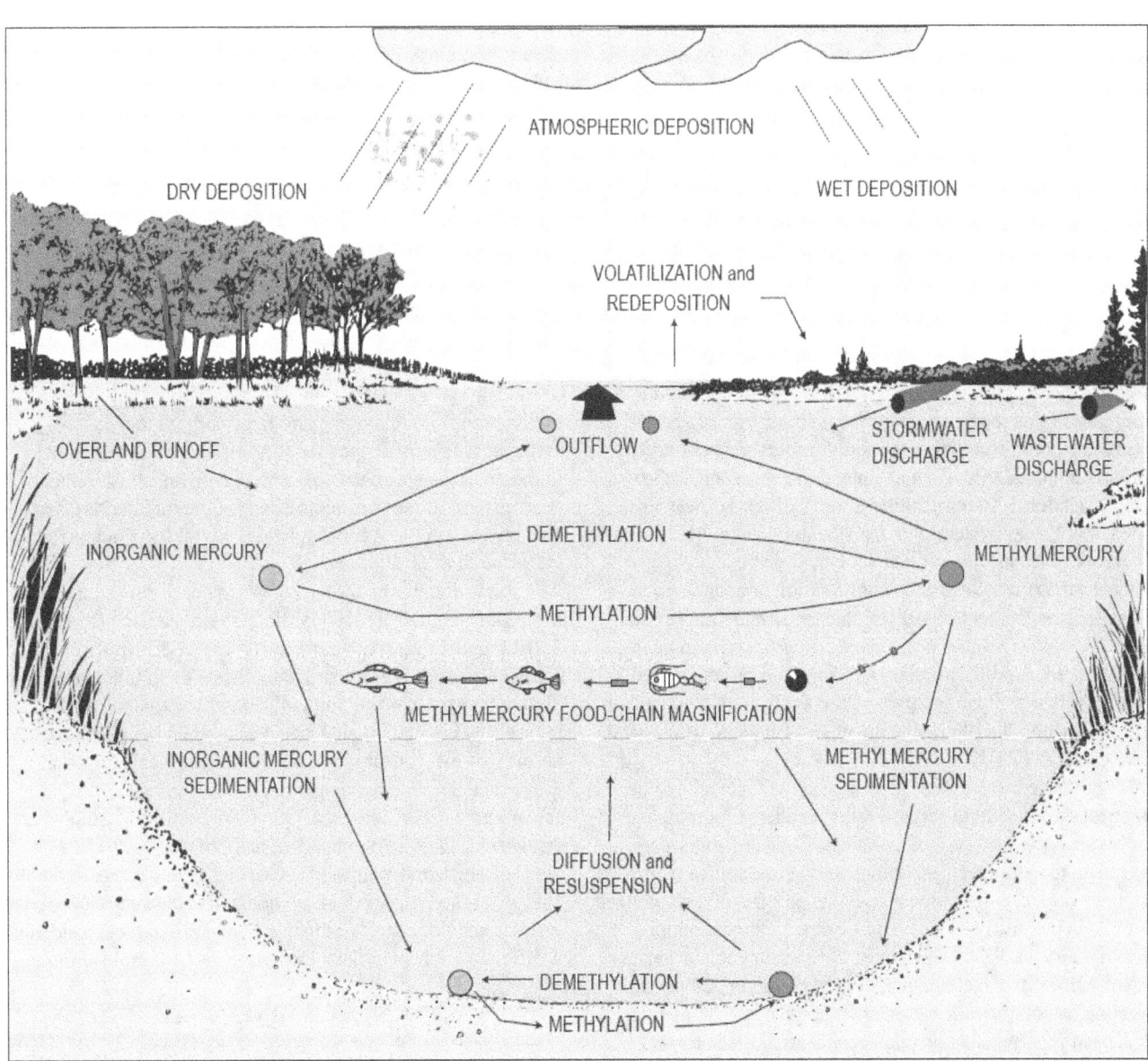

Figure 1. The mercury cycle in aquatic ecosystems (modified from Krabbenhoft and Rickert, 1995).

Health Effects, Criteria, and Advisories for Mercury

Very low concentrations (more than 12 ng/L) of total mercury in water can lead to concentrations of methylmercury in fish tissue that constitute a health risk. An important route of exposure to methylmercury for some humans and wildlife is eating fish from streams and lakes. Methylmercury is a potent neurotoxin and potential endocrine disruptor that can affect humans and wildlife. Infants and young children are believed to have a high susceptibility to the detrimental effects of methylmercury because their nervous systems are still in development (National Research Council, 2000). Adults also may risk adverse neurological and cardiovascular effects from methylmercury exposure (Mergler and others, 2007). Fish-eating mammals and birds exposed to high, environmentally relevant methylmercury levels can suffer reproductive and developmental impairments and reduced immunity (Scheuhammer and others, 2007). Populationwide effects in terrestrial wildlife also have been linked to mercury (Evers, 2005).

The U.S. Environmental Protection Agency (2001) freshwater criterion for methylmercury is based on the safe level for protecting human health from methylmercury in fish for consumption, which is a concentration of 0.3 mg/kg in fish tissue. The Indiana Water-Quality Standards list three criteria for total recoverable mercury (which is called unfiltered total mercury in this report and includes methylmercury). Statewide, the chronic aquatic criterion[1] for mercury is 12 ng/L to protect humans, animals, and aquatic life from chronic toxic effects (Indiana Administrative Code, 2007a). For water in the Great Lakes System, Indiana's human-health criterion[2] for mercury is 1.8 ng/L to protect humans from possible non-cancer effects resulting from consumption of aquatic organisms such as fish and shellfish (Indiana Administrative Code, 2007b). Also for water in the Great Lakes System, Indiana's wildlife criterion[2] for mercury is 1.3 ng/L to protect wild bird and mammal populations from adverse effects that may result from consumption of aquatic organisms (Indiana Administrative Code, 2007b).

Permitted wastewater discharges in Indiana are required to meet the applicable surface-water standards for mercury or obtain a permit variance, as of 2005.[3] The mercury permit variance focuses on pollution prevention and source control to achieve mercury-discharge reductions because of a recognized lack of economically viable end-of-pipe treatment options for mercury (Indiana Department of Environmental Management, Office of Water Quality, written commun., 2006). The availability of a permit variance acknowledges that mercury has been reported at appreciable concentrations in treated wastewater, as described in this report. Also, mercury in Indiana streams includes nonpoint-source contributions, primarily runoff and direct input from atmospheric deposition. For reference, concentrations of mercury in precipitation in Indiana were greater than the 12-ng/L criterion in 47 percent of 517 samples in 2001–2003 and in 41 percent of 441 samples in 2004–2005; nearly all samples exceeded the 1.3-ng/L criterion (Risch, 2007; Risch and Fowler, 2008).

Mercury has been detected in nearly all fish-tissue samples collected in Indiana since 1983 (Stahl, 1997), and the detected mercury is assumed to be methylmercury (U.S. Environmental Protection Agency, 1999 and 2009; Harris, Krabbenhoft, and others, 2007). Concentrations of mercury in some fish-tissue samples have prompted State health officials to issue advisories that limit consumption of sport fish caught in Indiana streams and lakes (Indiana State Department of Health, 2006, 2007). The annual Indiana Fish Consumption Advisory is based on the U.S. Environmental Protection Agency Reference Dose[4] and measured concentrations of mercury in fish-tissue samples collected throughout the State. This advisory recognizes a greater risk to some members of the population. The advisory can be summarized generally with the following statements. If advisory status is unknown, women (pregnant, breast feeding, or planning pregnancy) and children less than 15 years of age may assume that one meal of Indiana sport fish per month is safe. Women and children in this group should not eat any large carp, flathead catfish, walleye, sauger, or striped bass. Adult men and women not in the previous group may assume that one meal of Indiana sport fish per week is safe; however, some Indiana rivers and streams have "do not eat" advisories for all fish (Indiana State Department of Health, 2007).

According to the Indiana Department of Environmental Management (IDEM) (2006), mercury advisories affected 5,010 km (3,113 mi) of streams, 164 km² (63.5 mi²) of lakes, and 95 km (59 mi) of Great Lakes shoreline in Indiana as of 2006. Also according to the IDEM, 524 Indiana stream segments were classified as having impaired beneficial use because of fish consumption advisories for mercury. Each year, some 833,000 resident anglers 16 years and older spend 15.5 million person-days and $469 million fishing. An estimated 286,000 more resident anglers were 6 to 15 years old (U.S. Fish and Wildlife Service and U.S. Census Bureau, 2003). On the basis of these numbers, fish consumption advisories could affect approximately one of six Indiana residents.[5] A different survey (Indiana Department of Natural Resources,

---

[1] Criterion is a 4-day average concentration.

[2] Criterion is 30-day average concentration. The Great Lakes System in Indiana includes surface water in Lake Michigan and streams connected to Lake Michigan or Lake Erie.

[3] Indiana Administrative Code 327 IAC 5–3.5.

[4] The U.S. Environmental Protection Agency Reference Dose is 0.1 µg mercury per kilogram of body weight per day of exposure for women of child-bearing years, nursing mothers, and all children under age 15. The Reference Dose is 0.3 µg mercury per kilogram of body weight per day of exposure for women beyond their childbearing years and adult men (Indiana State Department of Health, 2006).

[5] The sum of 833,000 Indiana resident anglers over 16 years in age and an estimated 286,000 resident anglers 6 to 15 years in age is approximately 1.2 million Indiana anglers out of 6.3 million Indiana residents in 2006 (Indiana Business Research Center, 2009).

2007) reported that 92 percent of Indiana adult respondents were involved in outdoor recreation in the previous year and 52.3 percent of them participated in fishing, indicating they could be affected by fish consumption advisories.[6]

Description of the Study Area

Indiana is 92,947 km^2 (35,887 mi^2) in size, 38th in geographic area in the Nation. The estimated population of Indiana in 2006 was 6.3 million, 15th in the Nation, and children represent one-fourth of the Indiana population (Indiana Business Research Center, 2009).[7] Indiana has an extensive and abundant water resource that includes 57,410 km (35,673 mi) of rivers, 575 publicly owned lakes and reservoirs that total 430 km^2 (166 mi^2), 3,290 km^2 (1,270 mi^2) of wetlands, and 95 km (59 mi) of Lake Michigan shoreline (Indiana Department of Environmental Management, 2006).

The climate of Indiana is continental, influenced mainly by eastward-moving cold polar air masses and warm gulf air masses. The low-pressure centers formed by the interaction of these air masses are the major sources of precipitation in Indiana. Spring and early summer are normally the wettest periods of the year, as storm systems tap moisture from the Gulf of Mexico and travel across Indiana. Early fall is generally the driest period. Seasonal precipitation patterns vary statewide, particularly in the summer (when isolated thunderstorms are common) and winter (when lake-effect snows fall in northern Indiana). Mean annual temperature in Indiana is approximately 11°C (52°F) and ranges from 9.8°C (49.6°F) in the north to more than 12.7°C (54.8°F) in the south (Purdue Applied Meteorology Group, 2005).

The statewide average annual precipitation is 107 cm (42 in.) and ranges from 94 cm (37 in.) in northern Indiana to nearly 119 cm (47 in.) for southern Indiana. Snowfall (as liquid) accounts for 5 to 18 cm (2 to 7 in.) of the average annual precipitation, with the greatest amounts of snowfall in northern Indiana (Morlock and others, 2004; Purdue Applied

Meteorology Group, 2005). According to Clark (1980), approximately 68 percent of the mean annual precipitation in Indiana returns to the atmosphere through evapotranspiration, 24 percent enters streams and lakes through surface runoff, and 8 percent recharges groundwater. Generally, runoff is greatest in areas with steep slopes and relatively impermeable soils, which are characteristic of much of the southern third of Indiana.

In this report, watersheds are used to organize data for interpretation. A watershed, from a water-resources standpoint, is the area that gathers water from precipitation and delivers it to a stream. All streams have watersheds from which their flow is derived, including the flow during dry weather that comes from groundwater. There are two main watersheds in Indiana; one drains to the Great Lakes and the other drains to the Mississippi River (Clark, 1980). Approximately 10 percent of the land area in Indiana is part of the Great Lakes watershed—Lake Michigan and Lake Erie. The Mississippi River watershed in Indiana consists of two parts. The Kankakee and Iroquois River watersheds are approximately 8 percent of the State land area; these rivers flow to the Illinois River and then to the Mississippi River. The larger part of the Mississippi River watershed is approximately 82 percent of the State land area, consisting of the Wabash River watershed, the Whitewater River watershed, and minor tributaries of the Ohio River watershed; these rivers all flow to the Ohio River and then to the Mississippi River.

Purpose and Scope

This report summarizes and interprets mercury-monitoring data and the relation to mercury-source inventories and land-cover classes in 26 Indiana watersheds. Although it includes fish-monitoring data from the decade preceding 2006, the focus is primarily on the period 2001–2006. This report presents an inquiry into factors that influence mercury levels in Indiana watersheds. Atmospheric mercury—monitored in wet deposition in Indiana—is evaluated as an input to streams. Mercury sources—emissions to the atmosphere and wastewater discharges—are evaluated by their location, number, and mercury contribution. Land-cover classes grouped as land-cover types are investigated for their relation to mercury in watersheds. The report examines whether and where the mercury in fish of these watersheds was related to the mercury in the streams.

Environmental regulators, public-health officials, and natural-resource managers use data about mercury in the environment to design policies for voluntary and regulatory compliance with environmental-protection objectives and to assess the effectiveness of these policies. This report aims to serve their needs while also providing information for environmental scientists and interested citizens.

---

[6]The Indiana Statewide Outdoor Recreation Plan 2006–2010 (Indiana Department of Natural Resources, 2007) includes results from the Indiana Outdoor Recreation Participation Survey in 2003–2004, which found that 92 percent of Indiana adults responding to the survey said they were involved in outdoor recreation in the previous year; of that group, 52.3 percent participated in fishing. This survey, if representative of the state population, indicates approximately 4.34 million Indiana adults may participate in outdoor recreation (92 percent of 4.72 million adults) and approximately 2.27 million of these Indiana adults may participate in fishing (52.3 percent of 4.34 million)—which is approximately 48 percent of Indiana adults in 2006.

[7]According to the Indiana Business Research Center (2009), children less than 4 years in age (0.43 million) plus children 5 to 17 years in age (1.15 million) total 1.6 million of the 6.3 million total Indiana population (25.4 percent).

Methods of Study

A conceptual model was used to approach the data compilation and interpretation for this report:

- Mercury in stream water is related to streamflow and to what happens in the upstream watershed—atmospheric deposition, mercury emissions to the atmosphere, discharges of mercury in wastewater, and mercury retention and runoff in the watershed land cover.

- Mercury in the fish is related to mercury in the stream water.

In this report, a retrospective of mercury in Indiana watersheds is presented in the following progression:

- Total mercury and methylmercury concentrations in water from streams are summarized, compared with water-quality criteria, and examined for geographic differences and temporal patterns and trends. The relation to streamflow is explained. Stream loads and yields of total mercury and methylmercury are determined.

- The mercury concentrations in fish-tissue samples are summarized, compared with a water-quality criterion, and examined for geographic differences.

- The ways that sources of mercury potentially influence mercury concentrations in streams and fish from watersheds are surveyed with regard to atmospheric mercury deposition, mercury emissions to the atmosphere, discharges of mercury in wastewater, and land cover.

Sources of Data

The data used in this report can be classified as mercury-monitoring data, ancillary data, mercury-source inventories, and landscape characteristics. Monitoring data were compiled from national and state databases of water, precipitation, wastewater, and fish-tissue samples that had been analyzed for mercury. Collecting and interpreting information about mercury in the environment requires specialized techniques, tools, and knowledge. Care was taken to restrict the monitoring data to those documented to have ultraclean protocols for collecting, processing, and analyzing samples. These protocols include precautions to minimize the unintended introduction of mercury into the samples. The low-level mercury analysis techniques that were used achieved detections of mercury and methylmercury in water at concentrations less than 1.0 ng/L and concentrations in fish tissue less than 10 μg/kg. Ancillary data compiled for this report include streamflow and precipitation at selected locations that were used to estimate atmospheric and stream loads of mercury. Information from Federal

and State inventories of mercury sources were obtained, and maps of land-cover classes were consulted to help explain differences in mercury levels of Indiana's watersheds. In overview, the mercury-monitoring data, ancillary data, and mercury-source inventories include

- mercury concentrations in streams at 26 locations statewide, 2002–2006;

- instantaneous streamflow at the time of mercury sampling and daily average streamflow at or near these 26 locations, 2002–2006 (ancillary data);

- mercury concentrations in weekly precipitation samples at nine locations in Indiana, Illinois, Kentucky, Wisconsin, and Ohio, 2001–2006;

- daily precipitation amounts at 151 locations in Indiana, Illinois, Michigan, and Ohio, 2001–2006 (ancillary data);

- mercury concentrations in grab samples of wastewater from 64 publicly owned treatment works statewide, 2002–2005;

- mercury concentrations in fish-tissue samples from 502 locations statewide, 1993–2004;

- annual mercury emissions to the atmosphere and locations of stationary sources statewide, 2002 and 2005;

- locations of outfalls for permitted discharges of wastewater to streams statewide, 2005; and

- land-cover classes, 2001.

Mercury in streams.—Mercury concentrations were compiled for water samples collected from streams at 26 locations in a statewide network, 2002–2006 (fig. 2). The locations of 24 monitoring stations in the network were selected by the IDEM in 2002 to represent major watersheds, reservoirs, sources of water supply, urban wastewater discharges, special habitats, and areas with active and abandoned coal minelands. Two monitoring stations were added by the U.S. Geological Survey (USGS) in 2004. Twenty monitoring stations were located at bridges at USGS streamflow-gaging stations. The remaining six monitoring stations (stations 5, 6, 12, 17, 18, and 25) were within 2.7 km upstream or downstream from USGS streamflow-gaging stations.

During 2002–2004, the IDEM statewide reconnaissance of trace-metal and mercury concentrations in Indiana streams utilized 24 monitoring stations in the network. At these 24 stations, 3 to 4 times per year, IDEM collected grab samples of water that were analyzed for total mercury and methylmercury (Indiana Department of Environmental Management, Assessment Information System database, unpublished data, 2005). During 2004–2006, the USGS mercury monitoring

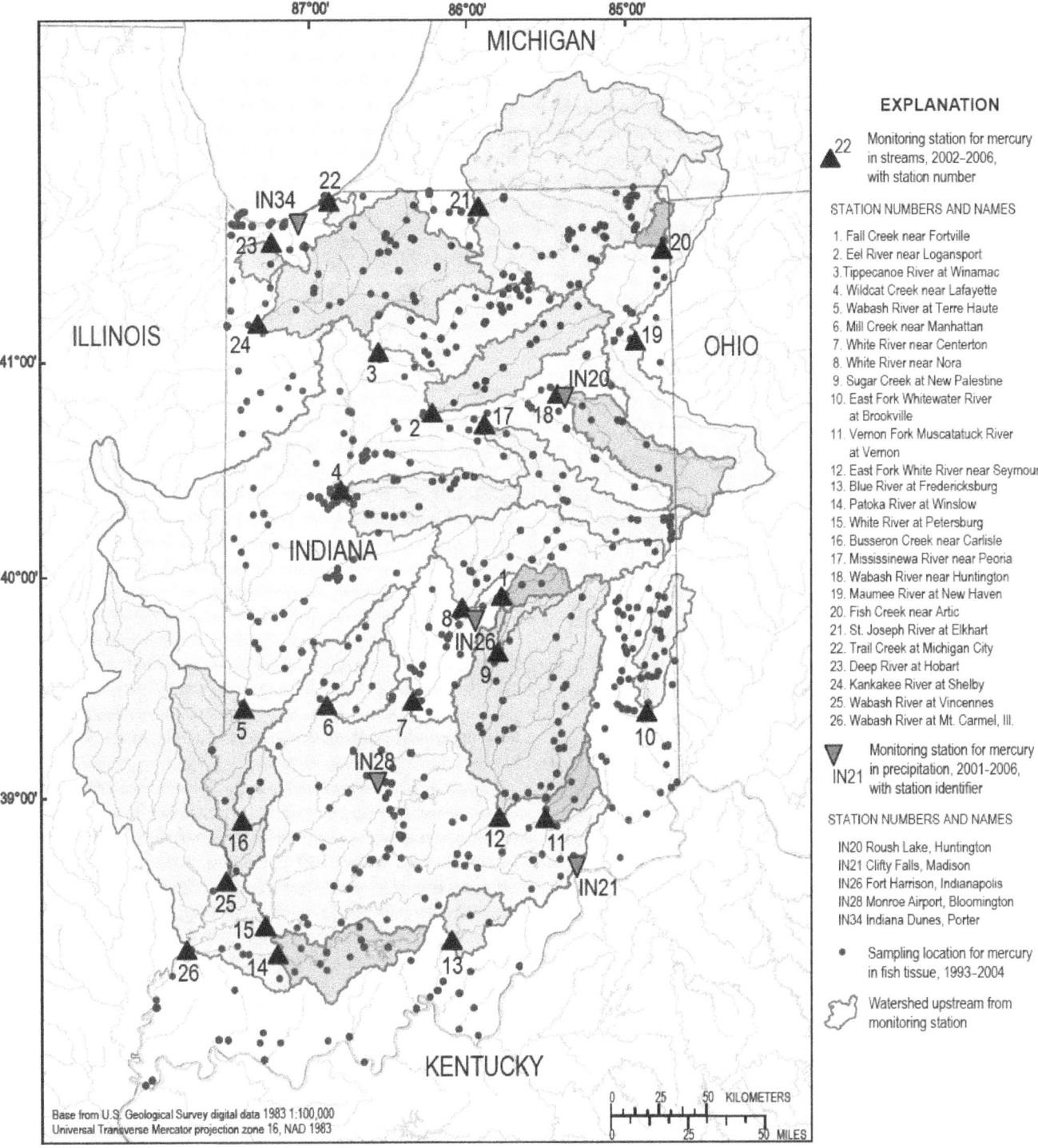

Figure 2. Indiana monitoring stations for mercury in streams, with upstream watershed boundaries, monitoring stations for mercury in precipitation, and sampling locations for mercury in fish tissue. (Some station names are slightly shortened in the list above and in most of the tables in this report. Full names are given in table 1.)

program utilized 23 of the 24 stations in the network, excluding station 26, and added new stations 15 and 25 for a total of 25. At these 25 stations, the USGS collected water samples once each season, using stream-width and streamflow-integrating techniques described in Ulberg and Risch (2008). Water samples were analyzed for total mercury and methylmercury at the USGS Mercury Research Laboratory (Middleton, Wis.), and the data for 2004–2006 are described in Ulberg and Risch (2008).

Mercury in fish.—The IDEM collected fish-tissue samples targeted to support the annual Fish Consumption Advisory that is prepared by the Indiana State Department of Health in collaboration with the IDEM and the Indiana Department of Natural Resources. The locations, species, sample characteristics, and total mercury concentrations for 2,225 fish-tissue samples collected at 502 locations statewide (fig. 2), 1993 through 2004, were obtained from the IDEM (Indiana Department of Environmental Management Assessment Information System database, unpublished data, 2005).

Mercury in precipitation.—Mercury concentrations and precipitation amounts in weekly samples were compiled for five stations in Indiana and one station each in Wisconsin, Illinois, Ohio, and Kentucky, 2001–2006 (fig. 3). These nine monitoring stations are part of the National Atmospheric Deposition Program (NADP) Mercury Deposition Network (MDN), which operated nearly 100 monitoring stations in North America by late 2006. At these nine stations, weekly composite precipitation samples were collected with automated samplers. The total mercury concentrations in the samples were analyzed by the MDN laboratory. Precipitation was measured with a recording rain gage. Mercury wet deposition (mass per unit area per time) was computed by multiplying the mercury concentration reported in each sample by the associated weekly precipitation. Annual mercury wet deposition was computed as the sum of the weekly mercury deposition. The study methods for Indiana also were used at the other four MDN stations outside Indiana. The study methods and data for Indiana are in Risch (2007) for 2001–2003 and in Risch and Fowler (2008) for 2004–2005. The data for 2006 in Indiana and for the stations in the other four states are from the MDN online archive (National Atmospheric Deposition Program, 2007a).

Mercury in wastewater.—Data on mercury concentrations in treated wastewater were compiled for 64 publicly owned treatment works (POTWs) in Indiana, 2002–2005 (fig. 4). The POTW operators collected 534 grab samples of wastewater that were analyzed for total mercury at private laboratories using low-level techniques. The samples were collected as part of an IDEM program directed at mercury in wastewater. The data for mercury concentrations in wastewater were archived in the U.S. Environmental Protection Agency Permit Compliance System database and retrieved for this report (U.S. Environmental Protection Agency, Region 5, written commun., 2006). Outfalls for permitted wastewater discharges, including all POTWs in Indiana, are part of a mercury-source inventory described in a subsequent section of this report.

Mercury emissions.—Information regarding stationary sources, nonpoint sources, and estimated annual mercury emissions to the atmosphere was summarized from the 2002 and 2005 Regional Air Pollutant Inventory Development System (RAPIDS) data for Indiana (Indiana Department of Environmental Management, Office of Air Quality, written commun., 2005, 2008). The 2002 and 2005 RAPIDS data include emissions reported by the owner or operator of the stationary source. Emissions from electric powerplants reported in RAPIDS had been calculated with an emission factor (for the type of coal and type of electric powerplant) multiplied by the amount of coal used as fuel. For this report, data have been summarized for stationary sources reporting annual emissions greater than or equal to 0.045 kg (0.1 lb).

In 2002, an estimated 4,604 kg (10,150 lb) of mercury was released to the atmosphere from 179 stationary sources; in 2005, an estimated 3,365 kg (7,418 lb) was released from 145 stationary sources. Among all types of stationary sources, the highest proportions of the estimated mercury emissions in Indiana were from coal-fueled electric powerplants, cement plants, and steel mills (fig. 5). The statewide distribution of stationary sources and their annual mercury emissions were not uniform (fig. 6).

Estimated mercury emissions from nonstationary/nonpoint sources such as gasoline and diesel fuel combustion in motor vehicles; natural gas, fuel oil, and wood combustion in heating units; human cremation; and miscellaneous human activities were 4 percent of all mercury emissions—191 kg in 2002 and 139 kg in 2005 (fig. 5). The mercury emissions from all sources in Indiana totaled 4,795 kg in 2002 and 3,504 kg in 2005.

Outfalls for permitted discharges.—Wastewater outfalls can discharge mercury to Indiana streams by channeling treated municipal and industrial wastewater, by diverting untreated stormwater runoff, and by mine dewatering. As of 2005, according to the Permit Compliance System database (Indiana Department of Environmental Management, Office of Water Quality, written commun., 2006), Indiana had issued permits under the National Pollutant Discharge Elimination System for 5,551 active and inactive wastewater outfalls, including 4,231 listed as active (fig. 7). Outfalls of a major facility have the capacity to discharge more than 1 million gallons per day. As these data are used in this report, a facility such as a POTW, industry, or mine can have multiple outfalls. All of the active and inactive outfalls were included because the time period of the inactive status was unavailable.

Land cover.—Landscape characteristics in Indiana were determined from 20 land-cover classes in the National Land Cover Database (NLCD) (Multi-Resolution Land Characteristics Consortium, 2001), which is based on satellite thematic-mapper imagery and supplemental data compiled with a 30-m resolution in 2001. Information on coal mine lands, which include active, reclaimed, and abandoned surface coal mines in Indiana compiled in 2000, was used to supplement the NLCD (Eaton, 2002; Indiana Geological Survey, 2002).

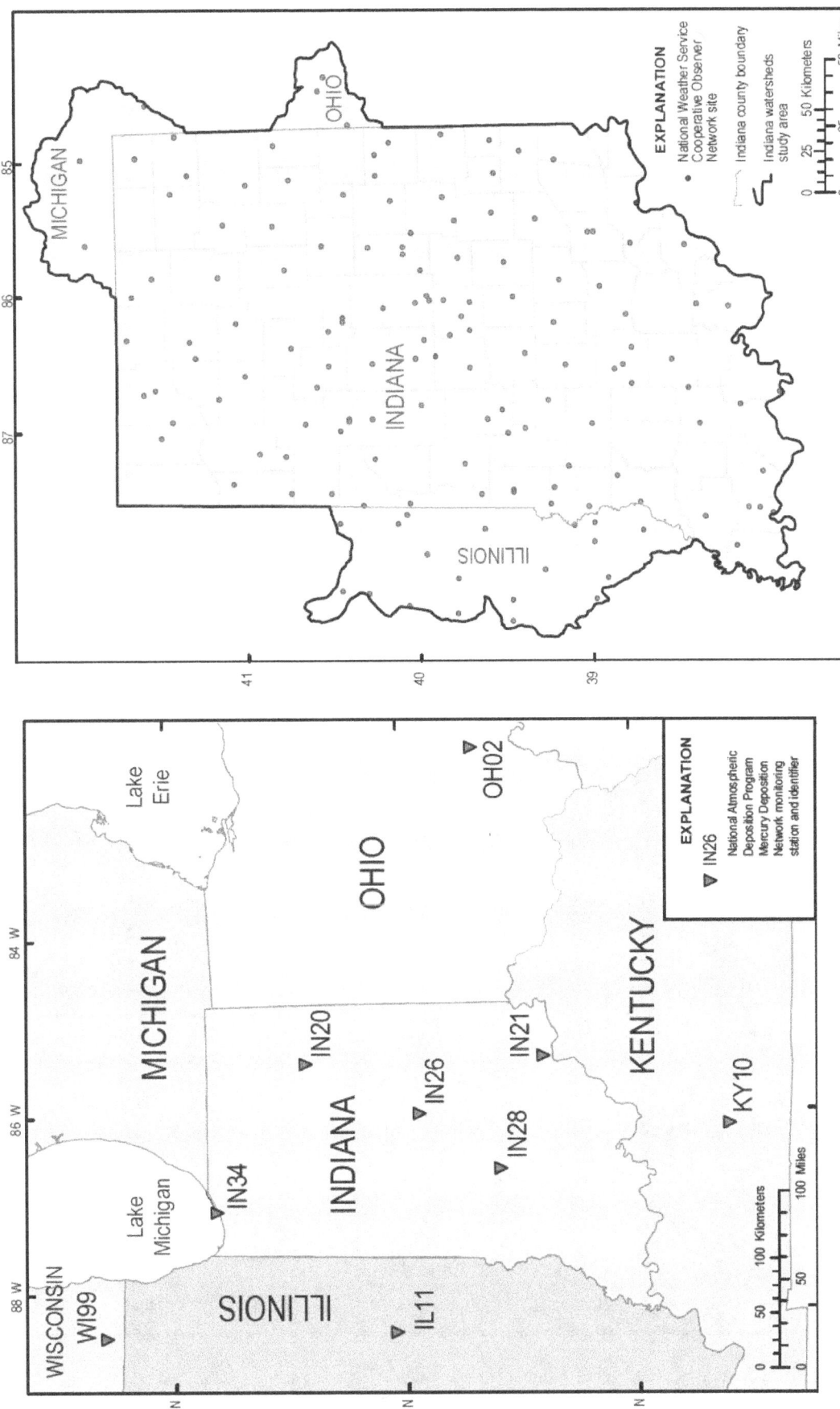

Figure 3. National Atmospheric Deposition Program Mercury Deposition Network stations used to compute average annual total mercury concentrations in precipitation in Indiana, and National Weather Service Cooperative Observer Network sites used to compute average annual precipitation in Indiana, 2001–2006.

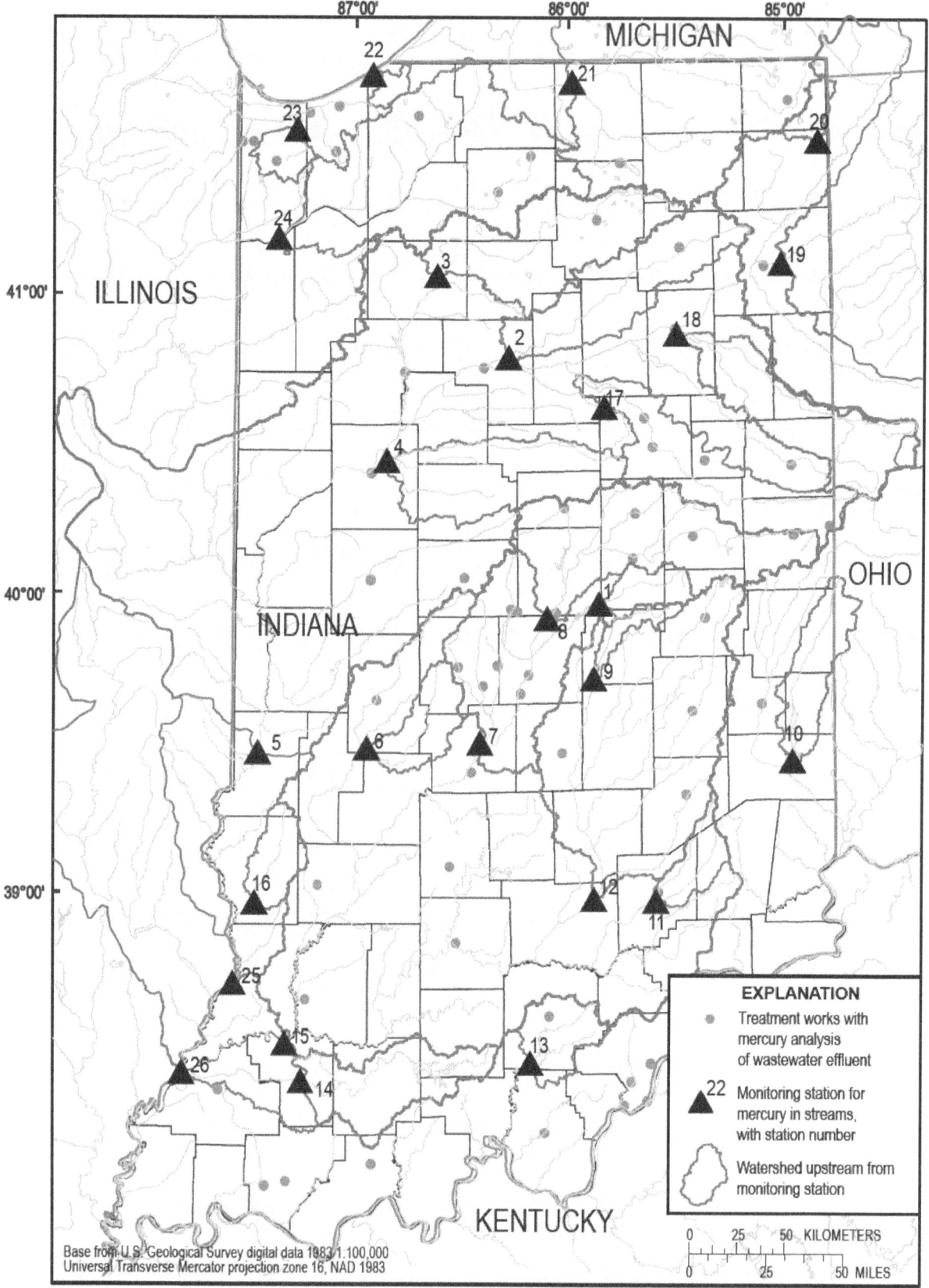

Figure 4. Treatment works in Indiana with total mercury analyses of wastewater-effluent samples, 2002–2005 (from U.S. Environmental Protection Agency Permit Compliance System); upstream watershed boundaries are shown for monitoring stations on streams.

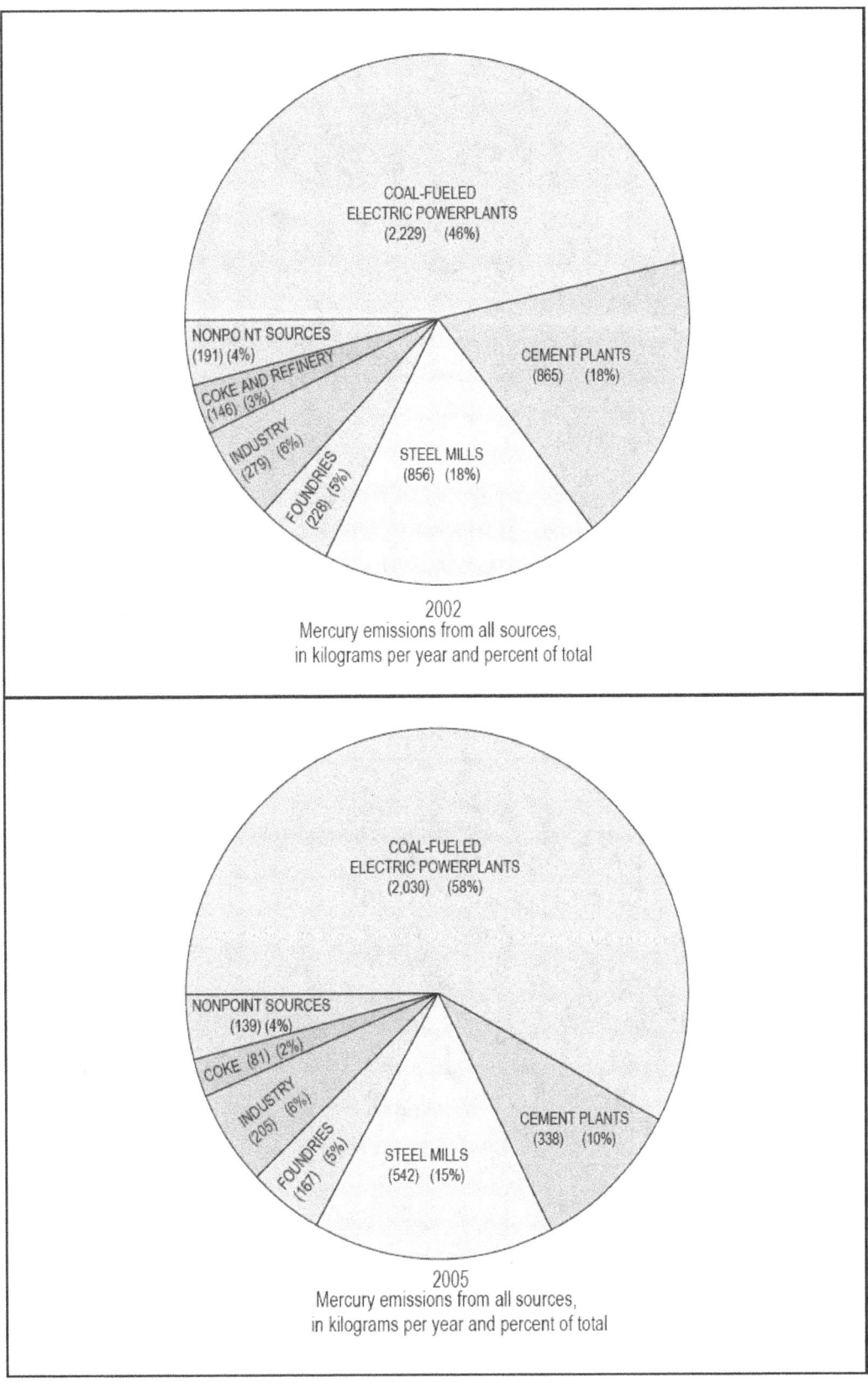

Figure 5. Annual emissions of mercury to the atmosphere from all categories of sources in Indiana in 2002 and 2005 (from Regional Air Pollutant Inventory Development System).

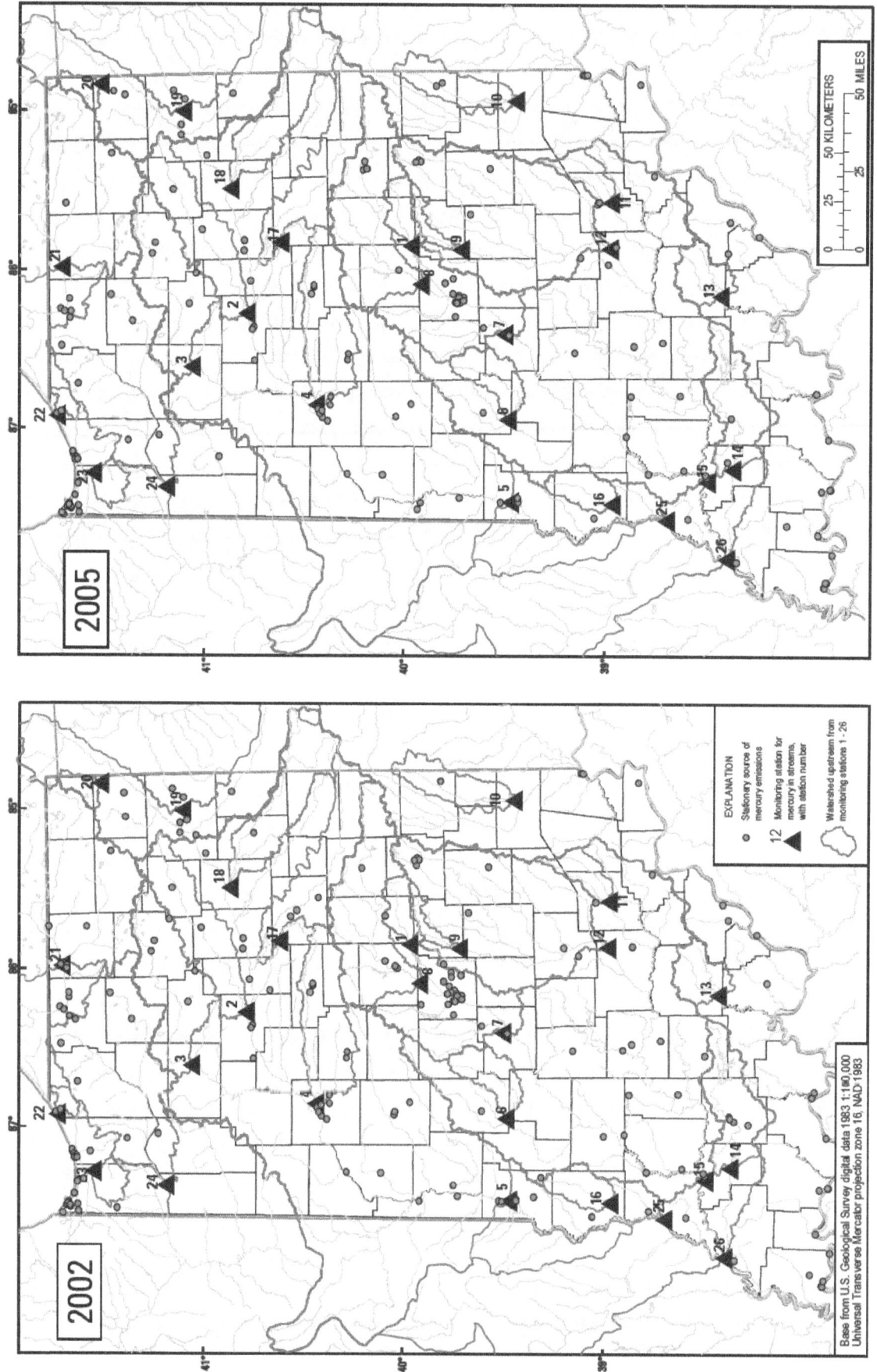

Figure 6. Stationary sources of mercury emissions to the atmosphere in Indiana in 2002 and 2005 (from Regional Air Pollutant Development System); upstream watershed boundaries are shown for monitoring stations on streams.

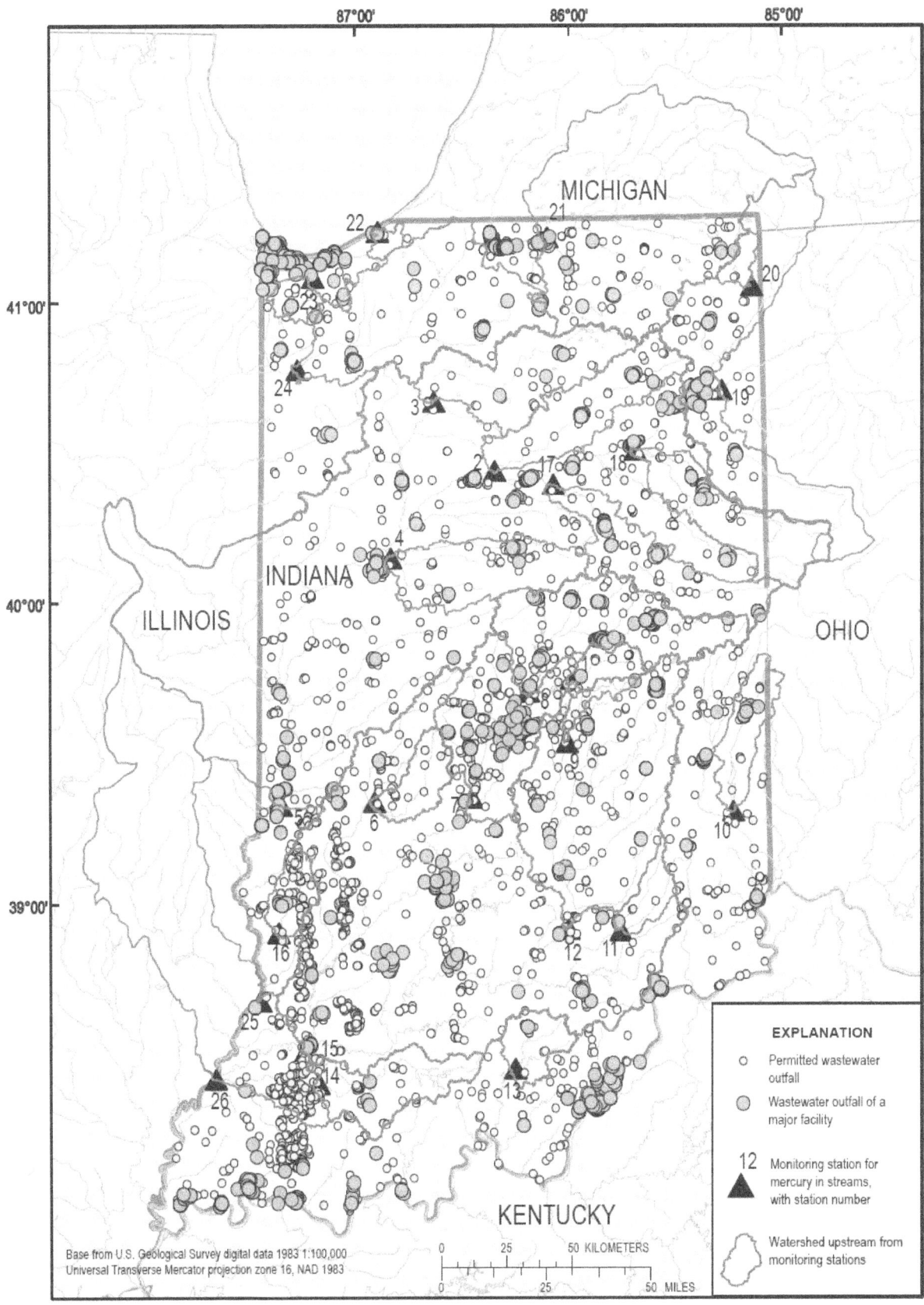

Figure 7. Permitted wastewater outfalls in Indiana in 2005 (from U.S. Environmental Protection Agency Permit Compliance System); upstream watershed boundaries are shown for monitoring stations on streams.

Organization of Data

Geographic information system (GIS) software Arc-GIS (Environmental Systems Research Institute, Inc., 2006) was used to organize the mercury data for this report. These data included point features and polygon features with their attributes. Examples of point features and their attributes are stream-sampling, precipitation-sampling, and fish-sampling sites with their mercury concentrations; and mercury-emission-source locations with their annual mercury emissions. Land cover is an example of a polygon feature with the attributes land-cover class and size.

A natural, hydrologic boundary was defined to group the point and polygon features. The boundary was delineated with the GIS as the drainage area upstream from each monitoring station. The 26 monitoring stations (fig. 2) had upstream drainage areas that ranged from 152 km^2 at station 22 to 74,293 km^2 at station 26 (table 1). The 73,919-km^2 combined area of these 26 watersheds inside the Indiana border represents approximately 79.5 percent of the land area in Indiana. Hereinafter, each of these upstream drainage areas is called a "watershed." The locations of the monitoring stations are identified by a station number (1 through 26), and this station number is also used in places to refer to the watershed. Two characteristics of these watersheds were taken into account during interpretation of data for this study: nested watersheds and watersheds that extend beyond the Indiana border.

In the case of "nested" watersheds, the watershed boundaries (fig. 2) for 12 of the monitoring stations lie within the watershed boundaries of 5 other stations (table 1). In some cases, a watershed is nested within other watersheds proceeding upstream. For example, the station 26 watershed includes the watersheds for stations 14, 15, and 25. The watershed for station 25 (which is part of the station 26 watershed) includes the watersheds for stations 5 and 16. Further upstream, the watershed for station 5 (which is part of the station 25 watershed) includes the watersheds for stations 2, 3, 4, 17, and 18. Some of the computations for this study, such as counting the number of sample locations or mercury sources, have to account for watersheds that are nested inside other watersheds upstream. "Unique" watershed areas that exclude the other watersheds nested upstream are used for these computations so that sample locations or mercury sources are counted only once. For example, the fish-sampling sites in the unique watershed area of station 5 excludes the fish-sampling sites in the nested watersheds for stations 2, 3, 4, 17, and 18 (fig. 2). Continuing the example, the calculation of mean annual stream mercury concentration at station 5 was not affected by the nested watersheds because the stream mercury concentration data for station 5 (and stations 2, 3, 4, 17, and 18) were site specific.

The 94,624-km^2 total area of the 26 watersheds in this study includes 20,705 km^2 (approximately 22 percent of total) outside of Indiana. The fraction of each watershed in another state is in table 1. In the case of watersheds that extend beyond the Indiana border, data from Illinois, Ohio, or Michigan were obtained if they were needed and available. For example, daily precipitation data for computing atmospheric mercury wet deposition were obtained for these three other states. Some interpretations, however, were made without data from other states, but the data were qualified as such. For example, data for mercury concentrations in fish-tissue samples and data on mercury-emissions sources and wastewater outfalls were not obtained for other states.

Statewide map layers of the mercury-monitoring data, mercury-source inventories, and land-cover classes were aggregated by watershed boundary for summary and interpretation. The GIS was used for a spatial analysis of attributes of polygon features in a watershed, such as the total area of each land-cover class. Specific attributes for point features were selected with the GIS, using logical expressions, and made into new datasets. The GIS allowed the original and new datasets, grouped by watershed, to be displayed in maps for interpretation and illustration. The GIS also was used to create atmospheric mercury wet-deposition isopleth maps and to estimate atmospheric mercury loads to the watersheds.

Mercury Load Calculations

Mercury load, rather than mercury concentration, is the measure used for comparing the amount of mercury delivered from a watershed with the amount of mercury entering a watershed. In this report, "stream mercury load" means a mass of mercury, per time unit, that was delivered from a watershed at the downstream end. Stream mercury load is based on the mercury concentration in the stream and streamflow. In this report, "atmospheric mercury load" means a mass of mercury, per time unit, that entered the watershed.[8] Atmospheric mercury load includes "mercury wet deposition," which is based on the mercury concentration in precipitation and precipitation amount. Stream mercury loads can account for the case, for example, where large streams with higher streamflow transport higher masses of mercury than small streams with lower flow, although the mercury concentrations in water samples from the streams are similar. Atmospheric mercury loads can account for the case, for example, where higher masses of atmospheric mercury are deposited in watersheds with the largest areas, although the mercury concentrations in precipitation and precipitation amounts are similar in the watersheds.

The following method was used to calculate stream mercury loads for Indiana watersheds, 2002–2006. A regression model for instantaneous stream mercury load was calculated with the program S-LOADEST (David Lorenz, U.S. Geological Survey, written commun., 2009), an adaptation of

---

[8] Atmospheric mercury input to a watershed by precipitation is wet deposition. Atmospheric mercury also can be input to a watershed by dry deposition of gaseous and particulate fractions or "species." Extensive monitoring data were available for mercury in precipitation, which is the reason this section describes the method to estimate atmospheric mercury wet-deposition loading rates. Mercury dry deposition data are limited for Indiana, but mercury dry-deposition are discussed in the section "Atmospheric Mercury Deposition."

LOADEST by Runkel and others (2004) written for S-Plus statistical software (Insightful Corporation, 2005). The regression model related the concentrations of unfiltered total mercury or unfiltered methylmercury from 15 to 18 quarterly water samples at each monitoring station during the 5-year period with the instantaneous streamflows at the time of sample collection. An option in the S-LOADEST program was used to rank predefined regression models applied to the data for each watershed, based on a set of criteria. The highest rank model with streamflow as the explanatory variable was used. The S-LOADEST program computed the intercept and coefficients for the equation of the regression model by means of the Adjusted Maximum Likelihood Estimate method. The daily average streamflow from the USGS streamflow-gaging station at or near each monitoring station (U.S Geological Survey, 2008) for calendar years 2002–2006 was input to the model. The program used the regression equation and these 1,825 daily average streamflow values to calculate a daily flux of mercury. The annual stream mercury load was computed as the sum of the daily fluxes for 365 days. The average annual stream mercury load for 2002–2006 was computed as the average of the five annual loads. Stream mercury loads were not calculated for some watersheds because of insufficient concentration data for total mercury (stations 15, 25, and 26) or for methylmercury (stations 1, 4, 8, 12, 15, 20, 21, 25, and 26); in some other watersheds, loads were not calculated because streamflow records included stream-stage control from dam structures (stations 6, 10, 17, and 18) or flow stagnation and flow reversals (station 22).

The stream mercury load from each watershed in grams per year (g/yr) was converted to "stream mercury yield" by dividing the load by the watershed area to give units of micrograms per square meter per year ($\mu g/m^2/yr$). Stream mercury yields enable watersheds of different sizes to be compared. The stream mercury yields for a watershed are reported in the same units ($\mu g/m^2/yr$) as the watershed atmospheric mercury wet-deposition loading rate (defined later in this section). See the "Mercury in Streams" section of this report for a discussion of the Indiana watersheds.

The following method was used to calculate atmospheric mercury wet-deposition loads and loading rates to Indiana watersheds, 2001–2006. This method is a modification of the traditional method used by the NADP each year since 2003. In the traditional method, data were used from MDN stations in North America where more than 75 percent of the weekly samples in a year were valid. The annual mercury wet-deposition rates at these MDN stations were computed as a product of the annual precipitation-weighted mercury concentration and annual precipitation (National Atmospheric Deposition Program, 2007b). The NADP used GIS software to illustrate one interpretation of the spatial distribution of annual mercury wet-deposition rates in North America, based on the rates at the MDN stations. The GIS software applied an inverse-distance-weighing algorithm to interpolate a deposition rate for each cell in a map grid of North America. At least two MDN stations within 500 m of a grid cell were required for a rate to

be interpolated. An isopleth map was made from the interpolated map grid. Isopleth bands generated by the GIS software spatially connected grid cells that had the same rates and represented 2-$\mu g/m^2$ ranges of annual mercury wet-deposition rates with different colors. These NADP isopleth maps are widely used and served as a starting point for load calculations in this report.

Maps of mercury wet-deposition rates for watersheds in Indiana, if derived from the NADP maps, would not have the desired level of detail required for interpretations at a watershed scale. The number and spatial distribution of monitoring stations is limited, and the deposition range in each isopleth is broad. For this report, a more detailed map of mercury wet-deposition rates was made with an alternate method. This alternate was based on the traditional method and incorporated data from 9 MDN stations and precipitation data from 151 National Weather Service (NWS) Cooperative Observer Program sites in and near Indiana (fig. 3). As in the traditional method, data from an MDN station or NWS site was included if more than 75 percent of the daily records per year were valid.

Making the map of mercury wet-deposition rates for the Indiana watershed study area required four steps. First, the average annual precipitation-weighted total mercury concentrations for 2001–2006 were computed for nine MDN stations (five in Indiana and four in surrounding states, fig. 3), by use of weekly monitoring data from each station. GIS software (ArcGIS, Environmental Systems Research Institute, Inc., 2006) was used to interpret the spatial distribution of mercury concentrations in the Indiana study area, based on the concentrations at the nine MDN stations. The GIS applied an inverse-distance-weighing algorithm to interpolate a mercury concentration for each cell in a 2-km^2 map grid of the study area. Second, the average annual precipitation, 2001–2006, was computed with daily precipitation values from 5 MDN stations in Indiana and from 151 NWS sites: 126 in Indiana, 19 in Illinois, 4 in Ohio, and 2 in Michigan (Midwestern Regional Climate Center, 2007). The 25 NWS sites outside Indiana were in the parts of 6 watersheds that extend beyond the State boundary. Third, a map of the 5 MDN stations and 151 NWS sites was overlaid with the interpolated mercury-concentration map grid, and a mercury concentration was assigned to every NWS site. For each of the 5 MDN stations and 151 NWS sites, the average annual mercury concentration was multiplied by the average annual precipitation to obtain the average annual mercury wet-deposition rate. Fourth, the inverse-distance-weighing algorithm was used to interpolate the spatial distribution of average annual mercury wet-deposition rates in the study area, 2001–2006, on the basis of deposition rates at the 5 MDN stations and 151 NWS sites. An isopleth map of deposition rates was made with the interpolated map grid. Isopleth bands generated by the GIS software spatially connected grid cells that had the same rates and represented 1-$\mu g/m^2$ ranges of annual mercury wet-deposition rates with different colors.

Table 1. Monitoring stations on Indiana streams, 2002–2006, and upstream drainage areas.

[km^2, square kilometer; NA, not applicable]

Station number	Station name	Latitude[1] (degrees, minutes, seconds)	Longitude[1] (degrees, minutes, seconds)	National Water Information System station identifier	USGS streamflow-gaging station identifier	Total upstream drainage area (km^2)	Unique[2] upstream drainage area (km^2)	Total upstream drainage area outside Indiana (km^2)	Total upstream drainage area outside Indiana (percent)
1	Fall Creek near Fortville, Ind.	39 57 17	85 52 03	03351500	03351500	447	447	NA	NA
2	Eel River near Logansport, Ind.	40 46 55	86 15 50	03328500	03328500	2,043	2,043	NA	NA
3	Tippecanoe River at Winamac, Ind.	41 02 59	86 35 57	03331753	03331753	2,438	2,438	NA	NA
4	Wildcat Creek near Lafayette, Ind.	40 26 26	86 49 45	03335000	03335000	2,056	2,056	NA	NA
5	Wabash River at U.S. Highway 40 at Terre Haute, Ind.	39 28 01	87 25 13	392801087251301	03341500	31,936	21,321	4,605	14
6	Mill Creek at tailwater pool near Manhattan, Ind.	39 29 11	86 55 08	392911086550701	03359000	759	759	NA	NA
7	White River near Centerton, Ind.	39 29 51	86 24 02	03354000	03354000	6,324	2,728	NA	NA
8	White River near Nora, Ind.	39 54 38	86 06 20	03351000	03351000	3,149	3,149	NA	NA
9	Sugar Creek at New Palestine, Ind.	39 42 51	85 53 08	03361650	03361650	243	243	NA	NA
10	East Fork Whitewater River at Brookville, Ind.	39 26 02	85 00 12	03276000	03276000	986	986	182	18
11	Vernon Fork Muscatatuck River at Vernon, Ind.	38 58 35	85 37 11	03369500	03369500	512	512	NA	NA

Table 1. Monitoring stations on Indiana streams, 2002–2006, and upstream drainage areas.—Continued

[km², square kilometer; NA, not applicable]

Station number	Station name	Latitude[1] (degrees, minutes, seconds)	Longitude[1] (degrees, minutes, seconds)	National Water Information System station identifier	USGS streamflow-gaging station identifier	Total upstream drainage area (km²)	Unique[2] upstream drainage area (km²)	Total upstream drainage area outside Indiana (km²)	Total upstream drainage area outside Indiana (percent)
12	White River at State Road 258 near Seymour, Ind.	38 58 23	85 55 46	385823085554501	03365500	6,056	6,056	NA	NA
13	Blue River at Fredericksburg, Ind.	38 26 02	86 11 30	03302800	03302800	732	606	NA	NA
14	Patoka River at Winslow, Ind.	38 22 49	87 13 00	03376300	03376300	1,559	1,559	NA	NA
15	White River at Petersburg, Ind.	38 30 39	87 17 22	03374000	03374000	28,794	14,854	NA	NA
16	Busseron Creek near Carlisle, Ind.	38 58 27	87 25 33	033342500	03342500	591	591	NA	NA
17	Mississinewa River at County Road 275 East near Peoria, Ind.	40 43 30	85 59 09	404330085590901	03327000	2,093	2,093	79	4
18	Wabash River at County Road 200 West near Huntington, Ind.	40 51 12	85 29 23	405112085292301	03323500	1,985	1,985	35	2
19	Maumee River at New Haven, Ind.	41 05 06	85 01 20	04183000	04183000	5,077	5,077	2,394	47
20	Fish Creek near Artic, Ind.	41 27 54	84 48 51	04177810	04177810	248	248	27	11
21	St. Joseph River at Elkhart, Ind.	41 41 30	85 58 30	04101000	04101000	8,756	8,447	5,030	57
22	Trail Creek at Michigan City Harbor, Ind.	41 43 22	86 54 15	04095380	04095380	152	152	NA	NA

Table 1. Monitoring stations on Indiana streams, 2002–2006, and upstream drainage areas.—Continued

[km², square kilometer; NA, not applicable]

Station number	Station name	Latitude[1] (degrees, minutes, seconds)	Longitude[1] (degrees, minutes, seconds)	National Water Information System station identifier	USGS streamflow-gaging station identifier	Total upstream drainage area (km²)	Unique[2] upstream drainage area (km²)	Total upstream drainage area outside Indiana (km²)	Total upstream drainage area outside Indiana (percent)
23	Deep River at Lake George outlet at Hobart, Ind.	41 32 10	87 15 25	04093000	04093000	321	321	NA	NA
24	Kankakee River at Shelby, Ind.	41 10 58	87 20 25	05518000	05518000	4,597	4,542	NA	NA
25	Wabash River at Vigo Street at Vincennes, Ind.	38 40 53	87 32 07	384156087310701	03343000	35,628	3,100	1,570	4
26	Wabash River at Mt. Carmel, Ill.	38 24 07	87 45 10	03377500	03377500	74,293	8,312	6,783	9

[1] Horizontal coordinate information is referenced to the North Amercian Datum of 1983 (NAD 83).

[2] Unique watershed areas exclude watersheds nested upstream.

To calculate atmospheric mercury loads to the 26 water-sheds, the watershed boundaries were overlaid on the isopleth map of average annual mercury wet-deposition rates. The mass of mercury in all of the grid cells within the boundary of each watershed was summed to yield the atmospheric mercury load for that watershed (in grams per year). The atmospheric mercury load was divided by the watershed area to provide an average annual atmospheric mercury wet-deposition loading rate for each watershed, 2001–2006 (in micrograms per square meter per year). See the "Atmospheric Mercury Deposition" section of this report for a discussion of the Indiana watersheds.

Mercury in Indiana Watersheds

Indiana watersheds exhibited geographic differences when mercury concentrations in water samples from streams, stream mercury yields, and mercury concentrations of fish-tissue samples were compared. Watersheds also differed in the percentage of atmospheric mercury loading that contributed to stream mercury yield. Some of the geographic differences appear to be related to mercury emissions, wastewater dis-charges, and land-cover types.

Mercury in Streams

This section describes and compares mercury concen-trations in water samples from monitoring stations in the statewide network, 2002–2006. Stream mercury yields from watersheds upstream from the monitoring stations are pre-sented. The section concludes with a discussion of studies of mercury in streams by other investigators and a comparison with the findings for Indiana watersheds, 2002–2006.

Two groups of water samples were combined for this study—186 samples collected and analyzed by IDEM, 2002–2004, and 225 samples collected and analyzed by USGS, 2004–2006 (table 2). The IDEM and USGS labora-tories analyzed unfiltered and filtered water samples for total mercury and methylmercury. Comparisons of mercury con-centrations in streams at the 26 monitoring locations for the entire time period were represented best in the determinations of unfiltered total mercury as compared with determinations of filtered total mercury, unfiltered methylmercury, or filtered methylmercury. There was no significant difference[9] between the unfiltered total mercury concentrations in the IDEM and the USGS samples (p = 0.356, generalized Wilcoxon test[10]). In contrast, concentrations of filtered total mercury, unfiltered methylmercury, and filtered methylmercury in the IDEM samples were significantly different from the USGS samples (p < 0.001, generalized Wilcoxon test). The difference in these three mercury determinations was at least in part due to the higher number of censored values (less than the laboratory reporting limits) for the samples collected by IDEM during 2002–2004 (table 2).

Unfiltered total mercury concentrations reported in the 411 water samples combined from the two groups had a median of 2.32 ng/L, and the maximum concentration was 28.2 ng/L (table 2). Boxplots showing the distributions of the unfiltered total mercury concentrations (fig. 8) indicate dif-ferences among the 26 monitoring stations that were signifi-cant (p < 0.001; Kruskal-Wallis test[11]). The concentrations in samples from station 19 (median 7.05 ng/L) were significantly higher than those in samples from 10 other stations (1, 2, 3, 4, 6, 9, 10, 13, 21, and 23; Tukey's test[12]). The concentrations in samples from station 7 (median 6.0 ng/L) were significantly higher than those from 9 of these 10 stations, the exception being station 23. The concentrations from station 14 (median 4.58 ng/L) were significantly higher than those in samples from 7 of these 10 stations, the exceptions being stations 6, 13, and 23.

The highest unfiltered total mercury concentrations reported in the 411 samples are defined here as the top 10 percent—41 samples with concentrations greater than the 90th percentile, 8.62 ng/L. At least one sample from 18 of the 26 monitoring stations had an unfiltered total mercury concentra-tion that was among the top 10 percent. Stations 7, 14, and 19 each had five or more samples with mercury concentrations that were among the top 10 percent (table 3).

For reference, the 411 unfiltered total mercury concentra-tions were compared to the three Indiana water-quality criteria for total mercury. The 12-ng/L chronic-aquatic criterion was equaled or exceeded in 5.4 percent of samples (22 of 411), including at least 1 sample from 13 of the 26 monitoring sta-tions. The 1.8-ng/L Great Lakes human-health criterion was equaled or exceeded in 59 percent of samples (242 of 411), including at least 1 sample from all of the 26 monitoring sta-tions. The median concentration at 16 stations exceeded this criterion (table 3, fig. 8). The 1.3-ng/L Great Lakes wildlife

---

[9] A significance level (α) of 0.05 or less was used to accept a statistically significant difference for the statistical tests in this report, including the generalized Wilcoxon test, Wilcoxon rank-sum test, Kruskal-Wallis test, and Tukey's test. The p-value is the significance attained by the data—the smaller the p-value, the lower the probability of incorrectly rejecting the hypothesis of no significant difference and the lower the probability that a significant difference arose by chance. The smaller the p-value, the more believeable the statistical difference.

[10] The generalized Wilcoxon test (Helsel, 2005) is a nonparametric proce-dure used to evaluate whether the distribution of data from the two groups was statistically different. It is a score test that assigns an estimated rank, or score, to each censored value. A censored value is one that is less than the labora-tory reporting limit, which means either the constituent was not detected or a concentration was not quantified.

[11] The Kruskal-Wallis rank-sum test (Helsel and Hirsch, 1995) is a nonpara-metric procedure used to evaluate whether the distributions of the data from more than two stations were different.

[12] Tukey's test (Helsel and Hirsch, 1995) is a parametric multiple-compari-son test of the means of the data for each station to determine whether there is a significant difference in the groups of data. Tukey's method is applicable to multiple comparisons of groups that are equal or unequal in size.

criterion was equaled or exceeded in 72.5 percent of samples (298 of 411), including at least 1 sample from all 26 stations and all of the samples from 6 stations. The median concentration at 20 stations exceeded this criterion (table 3, fig. 8). Three monitoring stations had high unfiltered total mercury concentrations:

    Station 7—White River near Centerton
    Station 14—Patoka River at Winslow
    Station 19—Maumee River at New Haven

These three stations (fig. 2) had the most samples with concentrations higher than the 12-ng/L, 1.8-ng/L, and 1.3-ng/L Indiana water-quality criteria, the highest maximum concentrations, and the most samples with concentrations higher than the 90th percentile (table 3).

On average, more of the total mercury in the water samples was in a particulate form than a dissolved form (fig. 9). The dissolved total mercury is the filtered total mercury concentration measured in water passed through a 0.7-micrometer (µm) nominal pore-size filter. Particulate total mercury concentrations were determined with uncensored values by subtracting filtered concentrations from unfiltered concentrations (n = 387). The percentage of particulate total mercury is the ratio of the particulate total mercury concentration to the corresponding unfiltered total mercury concentration.

For all stations combined, the average particulate total mercury values were 2.93 ng/L and 67 percent. The highest average particulate total mercury concentration was 7.35 ng/L in samples from station 7 (table 4); these samples had

Table 2.   Summary statistics for mercury concentrations in water samples from monitoring stations on Indiana streams, 2002–2006.

[ng/L, nanogram per liter; <, less than; IDEM, Indiana Department of Environmental Management; USGS, U.S. Geological Survey; N.A., not applicable]

Description	Unfiltered total mercury	Filtered total mercury	Estimated particulate total mercury[1]	Unfiltered methyl-mercury	Filtered methyl-mercury	Percentage of methyl-mercury[2]
Concentration						
Median[3] (ng/L)	2.32	0.56	1.74	0.10	0.07	3.7
Maximum (ng/L)	28.2	6.14	26.8	.66	.68	64.8
Uncensored values	410	387	387	252	129	252
Censored values[4]						
IDEM	1	23	23	121	172	NA
USGS	0	0	0	38	109	NA
Total	1	23	23	159	281	NA
Number of samples						
IDEM	186	185	185	186	185	106
USGS	225	225	225	225	225	146
Total	411	410	410	411	410	252

[1] Particulate mercury concentration was estimated by subtracting filtered concentration from unfiltered concentration for samples with both concentrations greater than the reporting limit.

[2] Percentage of methylmercury is the ratio of unfiltered methylmercury to unfiltered total mercury for samples with both concentrations greater than the reporting limit, expressed as a percentage.

[3] Medians for unfiltered and filtered total mercury and methylmercury include censored values and were computed with the Adjusted Maximum Likelihood Estimate procedure (Helsel, 2005) by use of statistical software (S-Plus, Tibco Software, 2008). Medians for estimated particulate mercury and percentage of methylmercury were computed with uncensored values.

[4] A censored value is one that is less than the laboratory reporting limit, which means either the constituent was not detected or a concentration was not quantified. A censored value is not a missing value. One IDEM sample was missing a value for filtered total mercury and methylmercury, which is reflected as 185 IDEM samples for those constituents, compared to 186 IDEM samples for unfiltered total mercury and methylmercury.

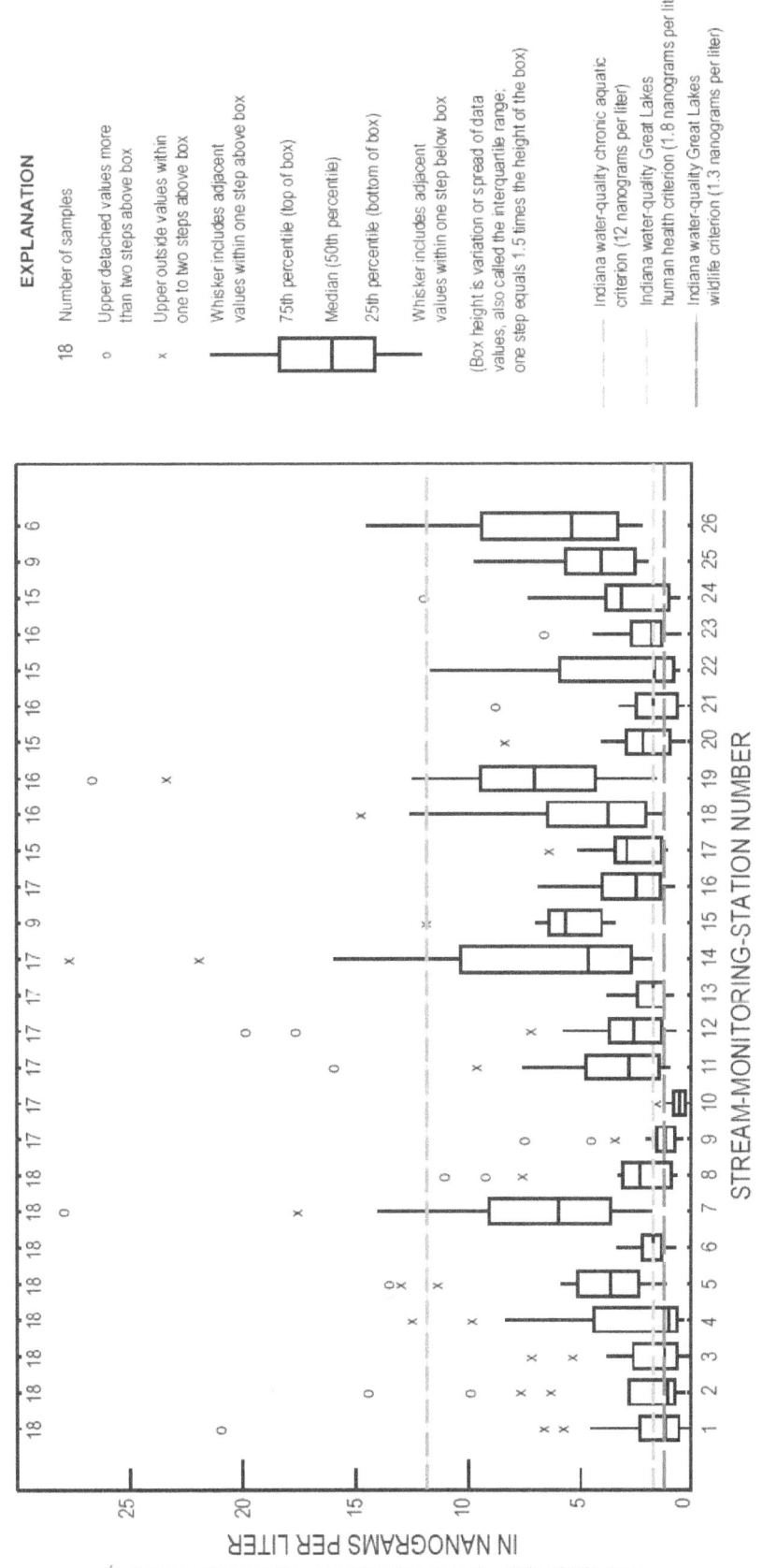

Figure 8. Distributions of unfiltered total mercury concentrations in water samples at monitoring stations on Indiana streams, 2002–2006. Locations of stream-monitoring stations are shown on figure 2.

88 percent average particulate total mercury. The percentage of particulate total mercury was highest in samples from station 26 (90 percent). The lowest average particulate total mercury concentration was 0.28 ng/L in samples from station 10, which is downstream from a dam. For all stations combined, the average filtered total mercury values were 0.91 ng/L and 33 percent. The highest average filtered total mercury concentration was 2.28 ng/L in samples from station 18, downstream from a dam; these samples had 39 percent average filtered mercury (table 4). The percentage of average filtered total mercury was highest in samples from station 10 (63 percent).

Other investigators have reported a positive correlation between mercury concentrations in water and suspended sediment (Brigham and others, 2009; Scudder and others, 2009). Suspended-sediment concentrations were not analyzed in the water samples analyzed for mercury during 2002–2006, so turbidity is used in this report as a qualitative indication of the level of suspended sediment. Turbidity measures the intensity of light scattering caused by suspended solids in a water sample (Wilde and Gibs, 1988). Suspended solids that affect turbidity include sediment particles, fine organic and inorganic matter, soluble colored organic compounds, plankton, and

Table 3. Total mercury concentrations in water samples from monitoring stations on Indiana streams, 2002–2006, with comparisons to Indiana water-quality criteria.

[>, greater than; ng/L, nanogram per liter]

Station number	Station name	Number of samples	Median concentration[2] (ng/L)	Maximum concentration (ng/L)	Samples with concentration[3] > 8.62 ng/L	Comparisons with water-quality criteria[1]		
						Samples with concentration > 12 ng/L	Samples with concentration > 1.8 ng/L	Samples with concentration > 1.3 ng/L
1	Fall Creek near Fortville	19	1.22	21.2	1	1	5	8
2	Eel River near Logansport	19	1.12	14.7	2	1	6	9
3	Tippecanoe River at Winimac	19	1.23	7.42	0	0	6	8
4	Wildcat Creek near Lafayette	19	1.03	12.7	2	1	6	8
5	Wabash River at Terre Haute	18	3.65	13.8	3	2	16	17
6	Mills Creek at Cagles Mill Dam	19	1.73	3.34	0	0	8	15
7	White River near Centerton	18	6.00	28.2	5	3	17	18
8	White River at Nora	19	2.36	11.3	2	0	11	12
9	Sugar Creek near New Palestine	17	1.21	7.74	0	0	4	8
10	East Fork Whitewater River near Brookville	17	.54	1.85	0	0	2	1
11	Vernon Fork Muscatatuck River at Vernon	17	2.80	16.2	2	1	12	14
12	East Fork White River at Seymour	17	2.59	20.1	2	2	11	14
13	Blue River at Fredericksburg	17	1.74	3.79	0	0	8	12
14	Patoka River at Winslow	17	4.58	27.9	6	3	16	17

microbes (American Public Health Association and others, 1992). Turbidity values do not correspond directly to concentrations of suspended solids or sediment, but these measures are typically strongly correlated. In this report, particulate total mercury is assumed to be adsorbed to or entrained in particles larger than 0.7 μm, based on the definition of dissolved total mercury presented earlier. These particles include sand, silt, and clay particles, excluding fine clay less than 0.7 μm (Horowitz, 1991). Turbidity values for 2002–2004 were from IDEM (Indiana Department of Environmental Management Assessment Information System database, unpublished

data, 2005), and those for 2004–2006 were from Ulberg and Risch (2008).

Particulate total mercury showed a strong positive correlation[13] with turbidity (r = 0.73, fig. 10). Turbidity of the water samples from the 26 monitoring stations, when classified by range, show that the distribution of particulate total mercury concentrations generally increases as turbidity increases (fig. 10). Nearly all particulate total mercury concentrations

---

[13] For this report, a strong positive correlation was indicated by a Pearson correlation coefficient greater than 0.70.

Table 3. Total mercury concentrations in water samples from monitoring stations on Indiana streams, 2002–2006, with comparisons to Indiana water-quality criteria.—Continued

[>, greater than; ng/L, nanogram per liter]

Station number	Station name	Number of samples	Median concentration[2] (ng/L)	Maximum concentration (ng/L)	Samples with concentration[3] > 8.62 ng/L	Comparisons with water-quality criteria[1]		
						Samples with concentration > 12 ng/L	Samples with concentration > 1.8 ng/L	Samples with concentration > 1.3 ng/L
15	White River at Petersburg	9	5.63	12.0	1	1	9	9
16	Busseron Creek near Carlisle	17	2.49	6.89	0	0	11	16
17	Mississinewa River near Peoria	15	2.89	6.65	0	0	10	12
18	Wabash River near Huntington	16	3.74	15.0	2	2	13	15
19	Maumee River at New Haven	16	7.05	26.9	5	3	15	16
20	Fish Creek near Artic	15	2.20	8.66	2	0	8	10
21	St. Joseph River at Elkhart	16	1.75	9.05	1	0	7	10
22	Trail Creek at Michigan City	15	1.67	11.7	1	0	7	10
23	Deep River at Lake George at Hobart	16	1.83	6.89	0	0	9	13
24	Kankakee River at Shelby	15	3.16	12.2	1	1	11	11
25	Wabash River at Vincennes	9	4.11	9.73	1	0	9	9
26	Wabash River at Mt. Carmel, Ill.	6	5.36	14.5	2	1	6	6

[1] Indiana chronic aquatic criterion (12 ng/L); Indiana Great Lakes human health criterion (1.8 ng/L); Indiana Great Lakes wildlife criterion (1.3 ng/L).

[2] Medians for unfiltered total mercury include censored values and were computed with the Adjusted Maximum Likelihood Estimate procedure (Helsel, 2005) by use of statistical software (S-Plus, Tibco Software, 2008).

[3] The 90th percentile of unfiltered total mercury concentrations in 411 samples, 2002–2006, was 8.62 ng/L.

exceeding the 12-ng/L Indiana chronic aquatic criterion were in water samples with turbidity higher than 60 nephelometric turbidity ratio units (NTRU).

Particulate total mercury concentrations at six stations were likely affected by impeded streamflow velocity, which can allow suspended particles to settle. Dams were within 4.3 km upstream from monitoring stations 6, 10, 17, 18, and 23; station 22 was subject to flow stagnation and flow reversal because of Lake Michigan influence. Particulate total mercury concentrations in samples from these 6 stations (n = 90) were significantly lower than those from the other 20 stations (n = 287; p < 0.001, Wilcoxon rank-sum test). The difference was significant when only the five stations with dams upstream were tested. The difference in median particulate total mercury in the two groups was twofold—1.01 ng/L in samples from the 5 stations with dams upstream compared with 2.02 ng/L at the other 20 stations. Ulberg and Risch (2008) reported a similar effect of significantly lower particu-

late total mercury concentrations from these six stations with impeded streamflow velocity in 2004–2006.

Unfiltered methylmercury as a percentage of unfiltered total mercury, called the percentage of methylmercury in this report, was computed for 252 samples from 26 stations where uncensored methylmercury and total mercury concentrations were reported. The percentage of methylmercury ranged from 0.4 to 64.8 percent, with a median of 3.7 percent. Station 6, Mill Creek at Cagles Mill Dam, had the most samples with concentrations above the 90th percentile, the highest median methylmercury concentration, and the highest median and maximum percentages of methylmercury (table 5).

Percentages of methylmercury in samples at the 6 stations with impeded streamflow that were identified previously (stations 6, 10, 17, 18, 22, and 23) were significantly higher than in samples at the other 20 stations (p = 0.031, Wilcoxon rank-sum test). The difference also was shown when only the five stations with dams upstream were tested. The median

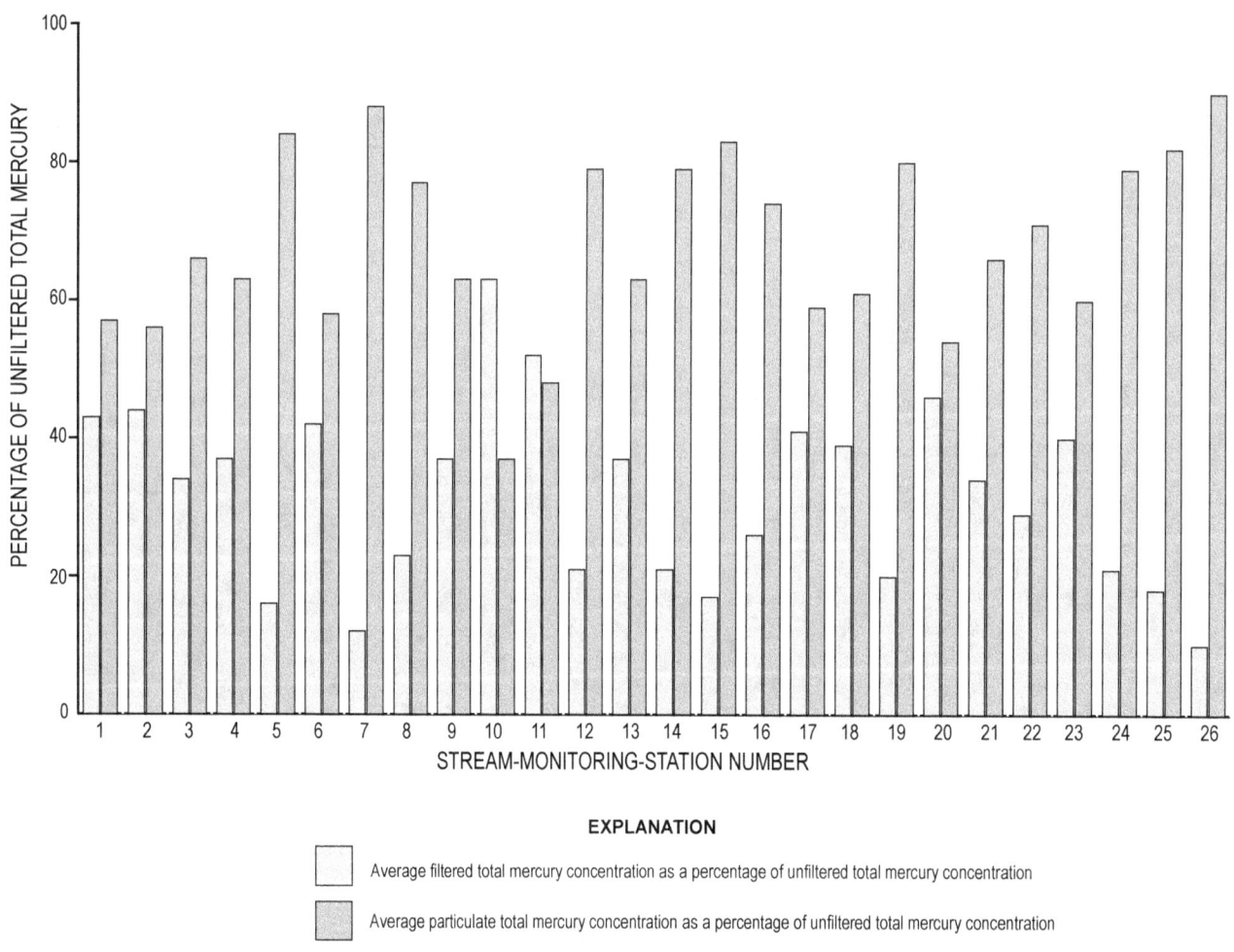

EXPLANATION

☐ Average filtered total mercury concentration as a percentage of unfiltered total mercury concentration

▨ Average particulate total mercury concentration as a percentage of unfiltered total mercury concentration

Figure 9. Average percentages of filtered and particulate total mercury in water samples at monitoring stations on Indiana streams, 2002–2006. (Locations of stream-monitoring stations are shown on figure 2.)

Table 4. Filtered total mercury and estimated particulate mercury concentrations in water samples from monitoring stations on Indiana streams, 2002–2006.

[ng/L, nanograms per liter]

Station number	Station name	Number of samples	Filtered total mercury		Particulate total mercury	
			Average concentration[1] (ng/L)	Average percentage filtered mercury[2]	Average concentration[1] (ng/L)	Average percentage particulate mercury[3]
1	Fall Creek near Fortville	18	0.64	43	2.15	57
2	Eel River near Logansport	18	1.02	44	1.96	56
3	Tippecanoe River at Winimac	18	.56	34	1.58	66
4	Wildcat Creek near Lafayette	18	.64	37	2.67	63
5	Wabash River at Terre Haute	18	.75	16	4.34	84
6	Mills Creek at Cagles Mill Dam[4]	18	.83	42	1.02	58
7	White River near Centerton	18	.77	12	7.35	88
8	White River at Nora	18	.67	23	2.82	77
9	Sugar Creek near New Palestine	17	.53	37	1.29	63
10	East Fork Whitewater River near Brookville[4]	17	.38	63	.28	37
11	Vernon Fork Muscatatuck River at Vernon	17	1.80	52	2.48	48
12	East Fork White River at Seymour	17	.78	21	3.91	79
13	Blue River at Fredericksburg	17	.70	37	1.17	63
14	Patoka River at Winslow	17	1.60	21	6.20	79
15	White River at Petersburg	9	1.02	17	4.82	83
16	Busseron Creek near Carlisle	17	.78	26	2.34	74
17	Mississinewa River near Peoria[4]	15	1.18	41	1.86	59
18	Wabash River near Huntington[4]	16	2.28	39	3.05	61
19	Maumee River at New Haven	16	1.76	20	7.10	80
20	Fish Creek near Artic	15	1.15	46	1.55	54
21	St. Joseph River at Elkhart	16	.54	34	1.75	66
22	Trail Creek at Michigan City[4]	15	.66	29	2.65	71
23	Deep River at Lake George at Hobart[4]	16	.93	40	1.36	60
24	Kankakee River at Shelby	15	.64	21	3.19	79
25	Wabash River at Vincennes	9	.84	18	3.70	82
26	Wabash River at Mt. Carmel, Ill.	6	.60	10	6.09	90

[1] Averages for filtered total mercury at each station include censored values and were computed with the Adjusted Maximum Likelihood Estimate procedure (Helsel, 2005) by use of statistical software (S-Plus, Tibco Software, 2008).

[2] The percentage of filtered mercury is the ratio of filtered to unfiltered concentration, expressed as a percentage.

[3] The percentage of particulate mercury is the ratio of filtered to unfiltered concentration, expressed as a percentage. Particulate total mercury was estimated with uncensored total mercury concentrations.

[4] Flow was impeded at station because of a dam or because of flow stagnation and reversal.

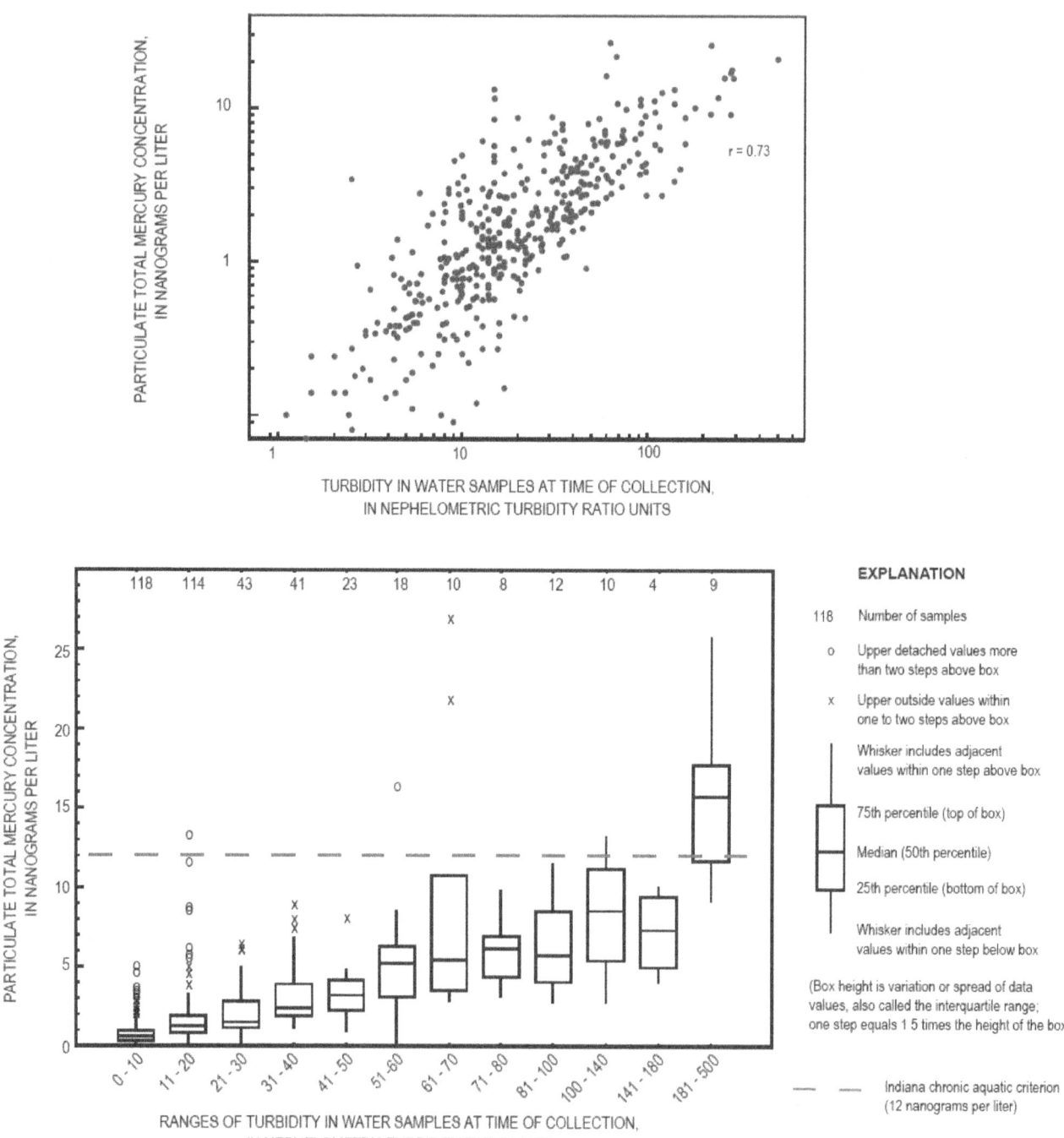

Figure 10.   Relations of particulate total mercury concentrations in water samples to turbidity values and ranges of turbidity in water at the time of sample collection at monitoring stations on Indiana streams, 2002–2006.

percentage of methylmercury for the group of 5 monitoring stations downstream from dams was 4.7 percent, compared to 3.6 percent for the other 21 stations. Ulberg and Risch (2008) reported a similar effect of statistically higher percentage of methylmercury at the six stations with impeded streamflow velocity in 2004–2006.

The degree to which mercury concentrations and turbidity in water samples were related to instantaneous streamflow at the time of sample collection varied considerably among the monitoring stations. A strong positive correlation of unfiltered and filtered total mercury concentrations with instantaneous streamflow was indicated for stations 1, 2, 8, 9, 11, 19, 20, 23, and 26 (appendix table 1–1). Particulate total mercury and unfiltered methylmercury concentrations generally did not correlate well with instantaneous streamflow.

Instantaneous streamflow at the time of sample collection was classified by assigning it to one of four categories[14] of daily mean streamflow for 2002–2006 (fig. 11; appendix table 1–2). Unfiltered total and filtered total mercury concentrations and turbidity were significantly higher when streamflow at the time of sample collection was in either the high or the event category rather than the low or the medium category (p<0.001, Kruskal Wallis test; Tukey's test).

For all unfiltered total mercury concentrations that exceeded the 12-ng/L Indiana chronic aquatic criterion, instantaneous streamflow was in the high or the event category. Median unfiltered total mercury was 3.2 ng/L at high streamflow and 6.8 ng/L at event streamflow; median filtered total mercury was 0.78 ng/L at high streamflow and 1.4 ng/L at event streamflow (fig. 11). Median turbidity was 21 NTRU at high streamflow and 36 NTRU at event streamflow. Ulberg and Risch (2008), using these streamflow categories, reported similar findings for total mercury concentrations and streamflow, 2004–2006.

The 411 water samples described in this report were collected on a seasonal schedule, and the unfiltered and filtered total mercury and unfiltered methylmercury concentrations and instantaneous streamflow at the time of sample collection were significantly different among the four seasons[15]—winter, spring, summer, and fall (p <0.001, Kruskal-Wallis test). Most of the seasonal pattern in unfiltered and filtered total mercury concentrations corresponds to seasonal patterns in instantaneous streamflow, whether flow-adjusted concentrations are used or not and whether data from six stations with impeded flow (6, 10, 17, 18, 22, and 23) are included or not. Total mercury concentrations and streamflow in winter and spring were higher than in summer and fall (p <0.001, Tukey's test). The median unfiltered total mercury concentrations in samples grouped by season were winter, 2.71 ng/L; spring, 3.28 ng/L; summer, 2.08 ng/L; and fall, 1.25 ng/L. Unfiltered methylmercury concentrations in spring and summer (medians 0.14 and 0.12 ng/L) were higher than in fall (median 0.08 ng/L).

Any 5-year statistical trend in total mercury concentrations would not confound interpretations of geographic differences. Five-year trends in unfiltered total mercury concentrations were examined by using the Seasonal Kendall test for trend (Hirsch and others, 1982).[16] The use of nonparametric procedures adjusted for serial correlation optimizes the sensitivity of the test for correctly detecting a significant trend. The median concentrations for the four seasons (winter, spring, summer, and fall) were used in the test because seasonal differences had been demonstrated. The test was made with data from each of the 26 monitoring stations and "statewide," combining 5 years of data from all stations (table 6). A significant trend of increasing unfiltered total mercury concentration was indicated for station 19 (p = 0.003) and station 8 (p = 0.035), but these trends in concentration corresponded closely with increases in streamflow. A significant trend in unfiltered mercury concentrations from all stations combined was not shown, whether data from the six stations with impeded streamflow (stations 6, 10, 17, 18, 22, and 23) were included (p = 0.482, n = 411) or excluded (p= 0.673, n = 314).

Annual stream loads of unfiltered total mercury and unfiltered methylmercury were calculated with data for 2002–2006 (appendix table 1–3). The method for determining stream mercury loads is described in the "Mercury Load Calculations" section of this report, and the characteristics of the load models are in appendix table 1–4. The standard error of prediction for the 89 annual stream loads of total mercury indicated that 4 out of 5 of the calculated loads were within 25 percent of actual loads; 64 of these 89 loads were within 10 percent of actual loads (appendix table 1–3). The highest uncertainty was associated with a standard error of prediction

---

[14] Instantaneous streamflow values for 2002–2004 were from IDEM (Indiana Department of Environmental Management Assessment Information System database, unpublished data, 2005), and instantaneous streamflow values for 2004–2006 were from Ulberg and Risch (2008). Daily mean streamflow category, for this report, was based on the daily mean streamflow record from the USGS streamflow-gaging station near each monitoring station for January 2002 through December 2006 (U.S. Geological Survey, 2008). For stations 15, 25 and 26, which had a shorter period of sample collection, the streamflow record for August 2004 through December 2006 was used. Daily mean streamflow categories were based on the rank-ordered daily mean streamflow data and are defined as "low" (less than or equal to the 10th percentile), "medium" (greater than the 10th percentile and less than or equal to the median), "high" (greater than the median and less than or equal to the 90th percentile), and "event" (greater than the 90th percentile).

[15] In this report, astronomical seasons in the northern hemisphere temperate zone are used, bounded by the winter solstice on December 22, vernal equinox on March 21, summer solstice on June 21, and autumnal equinox on September 22 (American Meteorological Society, 2000).

[16] The Seasonal Kendall test was developed by the USGS to analyze trends in water quality and has become the most used test for trend in the environmental sciences (Helsel and others, 2006). This test is a generalization of the Mann-Kendall test (Mann, 1945; Kendall, 1970) and reduces the effect that seasonal variations may have on trend detection by making comparisons of data from similar seasons (Schertz and others, 1991). The Seasonal Kendall test counts the number of increases and decreases in a parameter during a period of record, conducts the test within each season, and then combines the results from each season into an overall test for trend (Frans and Helsel, 2005). The direction of the trend is indicated by the Kendall's tau correlation coefficient. A negative tau indicates a decrease, and a positive tau indicates an increase. In this analysis, a significant trend is indicated by a p-value less than 0.05.

Table 5. Unfiltered methylmercury concentrations in water samples at monitoring stations on Indiana streams, 2002–2006

[>, greater than; ng/L, nanogram per liter; ND, not determined]

Station number	Station name	Number of uncensored concentrations	Samples with concentrations[1] > 0.29 ng/L	Median concentration of methyl-mercury[2] (ng/L)	Maximum concentration of methyl-mercury (ng/L)	Median percentage of methyl-mercury[3]	Maximum percentage of methyl-mercury[3]
1	Fall Creek near Fortville	8	1	0.07	0.29	4.4	11.6
2	Eel River near Logansport	10	0	.08	.27	4.2	17.9
3	Tippecanoe River at Winimac	8	0	.07	.19	4.6	9.9
4	Wildcat Creek near Lafayette	8	1	.08	.33	2.9	14.7
5	Wabash River at Terre Haute	14	4	.16	.66	3.8	30.5
6	Mills Creek at Cagles Mill Dam	8	4	.09	.57	16.1	64.8
7	White River near Centerton	15	2	.15	.29	2.2	4.4
8	White River at Nora	9	0	.10	.26	4.3	10.2
9	Sugar Creek near New Palestine	8	0	.06	.20	7.4	42.6
10	East Fork Whitewater River near Brookville	1	0	ND	.04	ND	15.4
11	Vernon Fork Muscatatuck River at Vernon	14	0	.11	.32	3.3	11.0
12	East Fork White River at Seymour	13	0	.11	.44	3.1	9.8
13	Blue River at Fredericksburg	8	0	.08	.20	4.4	10.8
14	Patoka River at Winslow	13	3	.12	.42	1.9	5.1
15	White River at Petersburg	9	2	.20	.41	2.7	9.9
16	Busseron Creek near Carlisle	11	0	.17	.22	4.9	6.5
17	Mississinewa River near Peoria	11	0	.09	.18	2.9	16.1
18	Wabash River near Huntington	14	2	.13	.66	2.7	15.4
19	Maumee River at New Haven	13	3	.21	.43	3.6	18.1
20	Fish Creek near Artic	11	0	.12	.26	7.9	15.4
21	St. Joseph River at Elkhart	8	0	.07	.12	4.5	12.5
22	Trail Creek at Michigan City	8	1	.07	.39	5.0	6.3

Table 5. Unfiltered methylmercury concentrations in water samples at monitoring stations on Indiana streams, 2002–2006.—Continued

[>, greater than; ng/L, nanogram per liter; ND, not determined]

Station number	Station name	Number of uncensored concentrations	Samples with concentrations[1] > 0.29 ng/L	Median concentration of methyl-mercury[2] (ng/L)	Maximum concentration of methyl-mercury (ng/L)	Median percentage of methyl-mercury[3]	Maximum percentage of methyl-mercury[3]
23	Deep River at Lake George at Hobart	9	0	.06	.15	3.6	24.5
24	Kankakee River at Shelby	8	0	.07	.13	1.9	4.2
25	Wabash River at Vincennes	9	1	.16	.42	2.3	16.5
26	Wabash River at Mt. Carmel, Ill.	4	1	.22	.33	2.7	14.9

[1] The 90th percentile of unfiltered methylmercury concentrations is 0.29 ng/L (n = 252).

[2] Medians for unfiltered methylmercury at each station include censored values and were computed with the Adjusted Maximum Likelihood Estimate procedure (Helsel, 2005) by use of statistical software (S-Plus, Tibco Software, 2008).

[3] Ratio of unfiltered methylmercury concentration to unfiltered total mercury concentration, expressed as a percentage.

Table 6. Seasonal Kendall test for trends in unfiltered total mercury concentrations in water samples from monitoring stations on Indiana streams, 2002–2006.

[ng/L, nanogram per liter]

Station number	Number of samples	p-value of test[1]	Kendall's tau[2]	Station number	Number of samples	p-value of test[1]	Kendall's tau[2]
1	18	0.068	0.438	14	17	0.878	−0.071
2	18	.325	− .250	15	9	1.000	.000
3	18	.482	.188	16	17	.878	− .071
4	18	.673	− .125	17	15	.382	− .273
5	18	1.000	.000	18	16	.744	.120
6	18	.888	.062	19	16	.003	.760
7	18	1.000	.000	20	15	.221	.364
8	18	.035	.500	21	16	.192	.360
9	17	.284	− .286	22	15	.600	− .182
10	17	.535	.179	23	16	.328	.280
11	17	.878	.071	24	15	.382	.273
12	17	.646	− .143	25	9	.245	.667
13	17	.284	.286	26	6	1.000	.000

[1] A statistically significant p-value is less than 0.05.

[2] The Kendall's tau correlation coefficient indicates the strength and direction of change for the trend. A negative sign indicates a decrease.

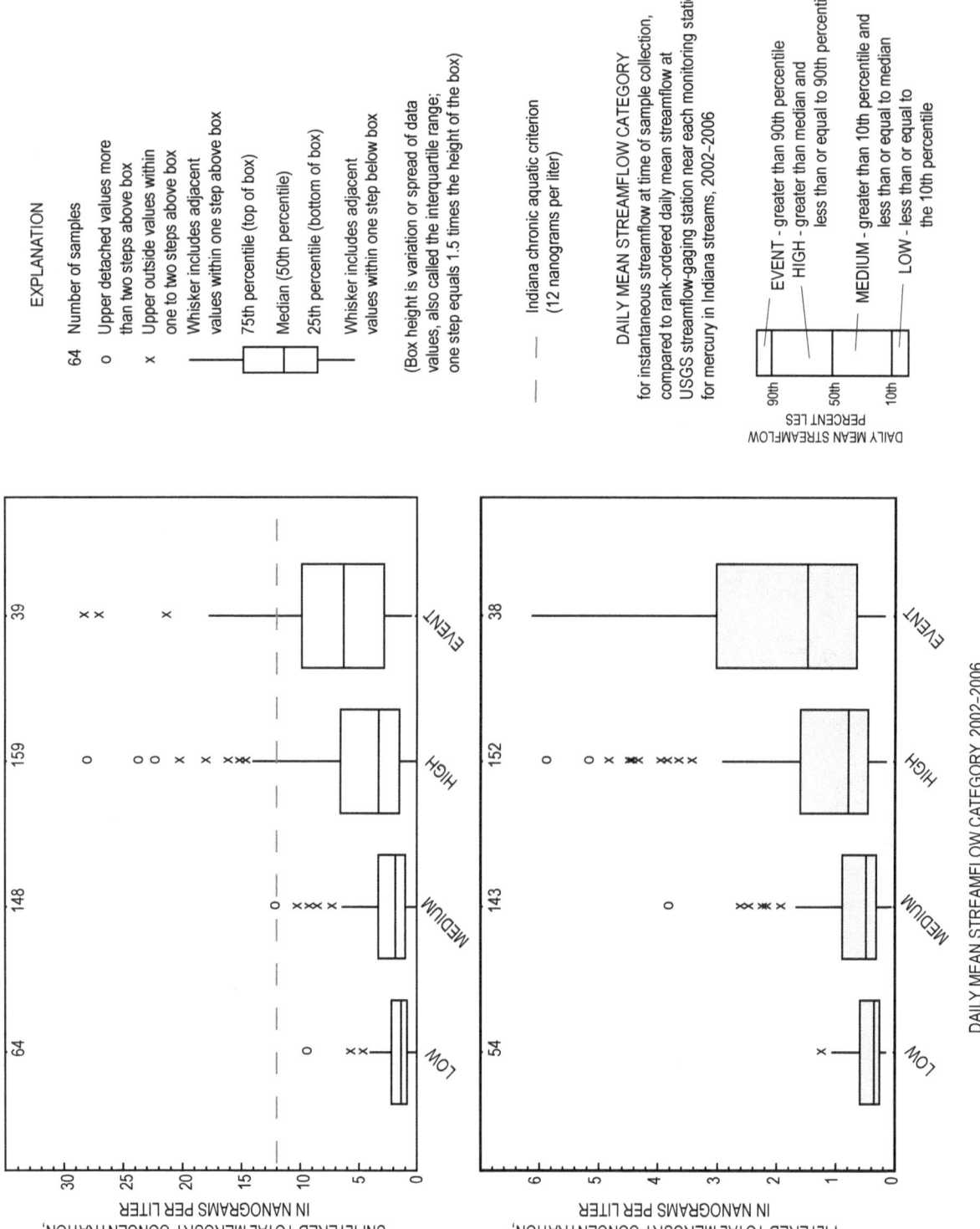

Figure 11. Distributions of unfiltered and filtered total mercury concentrations in water samples at monitoring stations on Indiana streams, grouped by daily mean streamflow category for instantaneous streamflow at time of sample collection, 2002–2006.

greater than 100 percent for six annual loads calculated for years that had one to three multi-day episodes of extremely high streamflow which were outside the fit of the load model. The standard error of prediction for the 54 annual stream loads of methylmercury indicated 49 of the calculated loads were within 7 percent of actual loads; 51 of these 54 loads were within 21 percent of actual loads.

The average standard error of prediction for the 18 average annual stream loads of total mercury indicated that 4 out of 5 of the calculated average loads were within 35 percent of actual loads (appendix table 1–4). The highest uncertainty was associated with an average standard error of prediction greater than 100 percent for two watersheds. The standard error of prediction for 10 of the 11 average annual stream loads of methylmercury indicated the calculated average loads were within 10 percent of actual loads.

Annual stream mercury loads were normalized to stream mercury yields by dividing the stream load by the watershed's upstream drainage area. Hereinafter, the term "stream mercury yield" will mean the normalized load, and a watershed will be designated by the monitoring-station number.

The 89 annual stream yields of total mercury from 18 watersheds ranged from 0.47 $\mu g/m^2/yr$ (watershed 21 in 2002) to 78.9 $\mu g/m^2/yr$ (watershed 12 in 2005); the median was 3.47 $\mu g/m^2/yr$. The 10 highest annual stream yields of total mercury ranged from 31.9 to 78.9 $\mu g/m^2/yr$; 5 of the 10 were from watershed 7 and watersheds 1 and 8 nested inside watershed 7 (fig. 12) and 4 of the 10 were from watershed 12 (appendix table 1–3).

The average annual stream yield of total mercury from 18 watersheds (table 7, fig. 12) ranged from 0.73 $\mu g/m^2/yr$ (watershed 21) to 45.2 $\mu g/m^2/yr$ (watershed 12); the median was 4.22 $\mu g/m^2/yr$. The highest average annual stream yields of total mercury were in:

Watershed 7 White River near Centerton (39.6 $\mu g/m^2/yr$)

Watershed 12–East Fork White River at Seymour (45.2 $\mu g/m^2/yr$)

The annual stream total mercury loads and yields from the 18 watersheds were significantly different (p <0.001, Kruskal-Wallis test). The average annual stream yields of total mercury indicate these differences are substantial. For example, the yield from watershed 12 (45.2 $\mu g/m^2/yr$) is approximately 63 times the yield from watershed 21 (0.73 $\mu g/m^2/yr$).

In 11 watersheds combined, the median annual stream yield of methylmercury was 1.9 percent of the median annual stream yield of total mercury. The 54 annual stream yields of methylmercury from 11 watersheds ranged from 0.03 $\mu g/m^2/yr$ (watersheds 3, 1, and 23) to 0.18 $\mu g/m^2/yr$ (watershed 16 in 2006); the median was 0.07 $\mu g/m^2/yr$ (appendix table 1–3). The average annual stream yield of methylmercury from 11 watersheds (table 7) ranged from 0.03 $\mu g/m^2/yr$ (watershed 23) to 0.12 $\mu g/m^2/yr$ (watershed 16); the median was 0.07 $\mu g/m^2/yr$.

The following discussion highlights conclusions from other investigations of mercury in streams and ties them to observations from Indiana presented in this report. In an overview, Ulberg and Risch (2008) summarized previous studies of mercury in U.S. streams that were done at multiple scales and compared the findings of those studies to mercury concentrations in Indiana streams, 2004–2006.

Total mercury and particulate mercury concentrations in Midwestern streams have been shown to be related predominantly to levels of particulates and suspended sediment. The mercury concentrations increase when streamflow increases because of storm runoff and snowmelt (Balogh and others, 1997; Babiarz and others, 1998; Hurley and others, 1998; Risch, 2005; Ulberg and Risch, 2008). In addition, mercury transport is often episodic and tied to streamflow and season (Schuster and others, 2007; Shanley and others, 2008). In a multiyear study of U.S. streams in different settings, Brigham and others (2009) concluded that particulate total mercury and methylmercury concentrations were positively correlated with streamflow. They also reported that (whole-water) total mercury and methylmercury concentrations[17] correlated strongly with dissolved organic carbon and suspended-sediment concentrations (data that were unavailable for interpretation of the 2002–2006 Indiana mercury data). Walling (1983) reported that a limitation of comparing constituent yields among watersheds of widely different upstream drainage areas is that many constituent yields, such as those for suspended sediment, tend to decrease substantially as the upstream drainage area increases. Understanding particulate mercury transport may be confounded by this limitation.

In a study of mercury cycling in different environments, Shanley and others (2008) determined that methylmercury tracked total mercury at a fairly constant ratio. They proposed that methylmercury production occurs in wetlands, riparian areas, and instream sediments where total mercury is sequestered in conditions that promote methylation. These areas for methylmercury production are hydraulically connected to streams and allow the methylmercury to be transported when storms cause increased streamflow. Brigham and others (2009) and Marvin-DiPasquale and others (2009) concluded that methylmercury production in stream-channel sediments was not important to the methylmercury load in the watershed. Rather, methylmercury in streams is predominantly produced in hydrologically connected wetlands and delivered in runoff to the streams. Similarly, Scudder and others (2009), in a national study of streams sampled during low flow, reported a positive correlation of methylmercury concentrations in water with total mercury concentrations in water, dissolved organic carbon, and percentage of wetlands relative to total land cover within the watershed.

Other investigators have reported that dams and impoundments increase methylmercury concentrations and percentages of methylmercury in water samples from reservoirs. Methylmercury concentrations in water from new reservoirs increases because organic carbon from inundated

---

[17] Brigham and others (2009) reported whole-water concentration as the sum of filtered and particulate concentrations, which are similar to the unfiltered concentrations in this report.

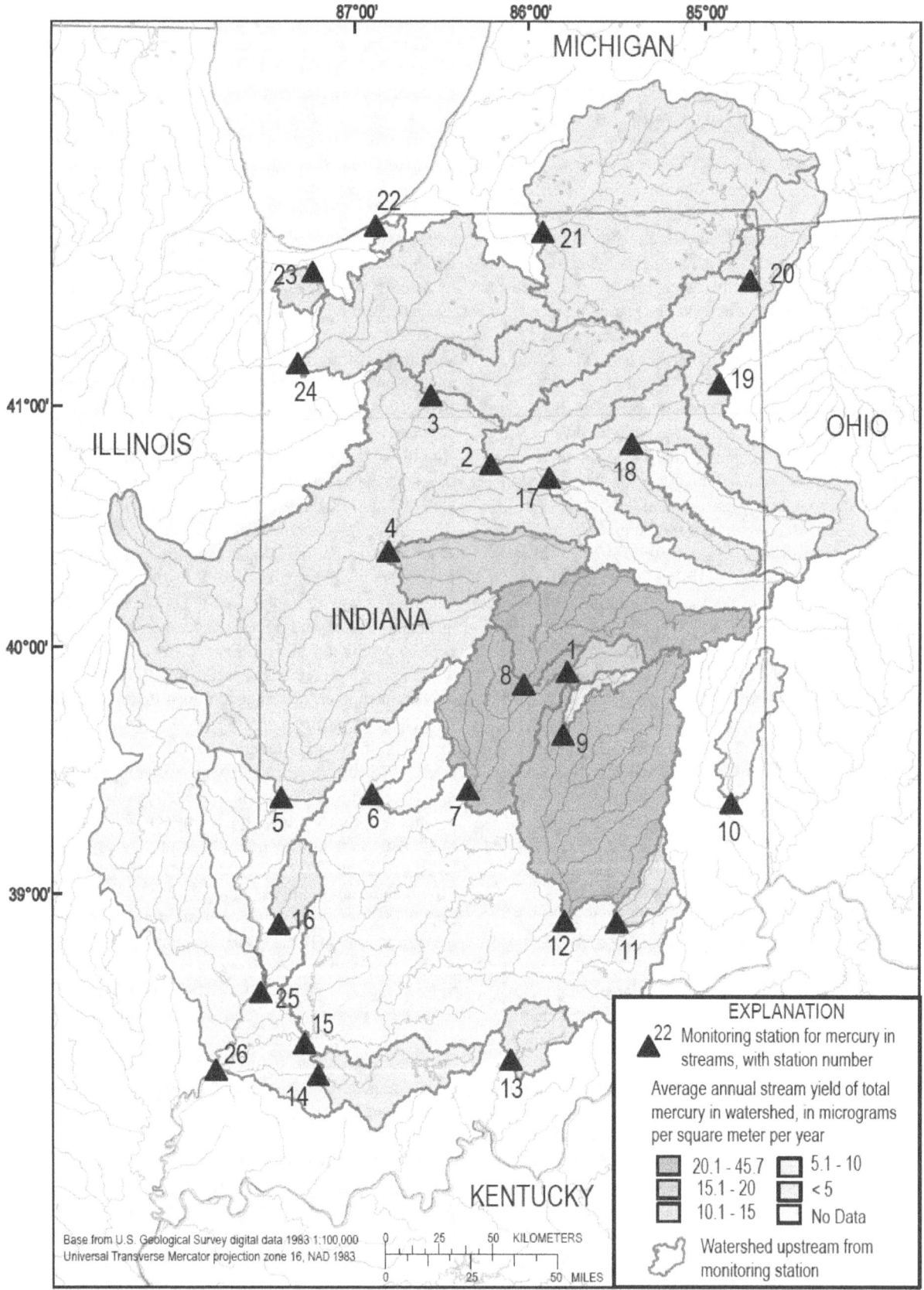

Figure 12.   Average annual stream yields of total mercury in watersheds upstream from monitoring stations on Indiana streams, 2002–2006.

forest soils and wetlands stimulate microorganisms that methylate inorganic mercury that is present (Bodaly and others, 2004). Decomposition of the organic carbon promotes anoxic conditions that favor microorganisms involved with methylation. Elevated methylmercury may persist for many years after a reservoir is first flooded (Hall and others, 2005; Bodaly and others, 2007). Methylmercury in the water is taken up by phytoplankton and zooplankton, in early years as dissolved methylmercury released from soils and in later years from methylmercury in resuspended fine particles (Plourde and others, 1997). Reservoirs with fluctuating water levels create periodic reduction and oxidation conditions that create and release methylmercury into the water (Kelly and others, 1997; St. Louis and others, 2004). Seasonal thermal stratification in reservoirs with a hypolimnion that is anoxic is thought to encourage methylmercury formation in the deep, anoxic water and shallow sediments; this methylmercury becomes vertically mixed into all the water during thermal destratification (Alpers and others, 2008).

With the knowledge from these other investigators, the following observations are made about the mercury-in-streams data for Indiana.

- Unfiltered total mercury concentrations in streams without impeded streamflow were predominantly particulate mercury. When streamflow was highest, unfiltered and filtered total mercury concentrations were highest. Turbidity of water, a surrogate for suspended particulates and sediment in water, increased as streamflow increased. Total mercury concentrations were highest in winter and spring, as was streamflow. Total mercury concentrations did not show a temporal trend during 2002–2006. Continuation of the seasonal monitoring of mercury in streams has the potential to detect long-term trends with underlying seasonal patterns and to identify geographic differences among watersheds and regions of the State.

- Mercury concentrations in streams had a 3.7 median percentage of methylmercury. Median annual stream yields of unfiltered methylmercury were 1.9 percent of median annual stream yields of unfiltered total mercury. Methylmercury concentrations were highest in summer and fall but were not related to available water-quality or streamflow information for Indiana streams. Methylmercury data for this report included a substantial number of censored values, which limited interpretations of percentage methylmercury and stream yields of methylmercury. A consistent laboratory reporting limit of 0.05 ng/L for all mercury analyses would have resulted in a better dataset.

- As shown by other investigators, mercury data for streambed sediments associated with the mercury data for stream water is unlikely to explain the source of methylmercury in the streams. However, data for dissolved organic carbon and suspended-sediment concentrations associated with water samples analyzed for mercury in Indiana could be useful for interpreting differences in total mercury and methylmercury among watersheds.

- Dams and impoundments increased the percentage of methylmercury in waters downstream and lowered the percentage of particulate total mercury during 2002–2006. As reported in other studies, reservoirs of various ages are likely to have conditions that increase the production of methylmercury. The methylmercury concentrations and percentages of methylmercury can be highest in the hypolimnion during summer thermal stratification, or they can be mixed in the water at other times. The effect of methylmercury on food chains and sport fish in reservoirs and downstream from reservoirs can be important. Investigations of mercury in Indiana reservoirs could help to explain the high percentages of methylmercury downstream from some of them and may provide information useful for natural-resources management.

- Stream mercury loads and yields were not meaningful for locations with impeded streamflow and potentially were confounded by large upstream drainage areas. A revised network of stream-monitoring locations without impeded streamflow and more uniform upstream drainage areas could improve capabilities for estimating stream mercury loads and yields.

Table 7.   Average annual stream loads and yields of unfiltered total mercury and unfiltered methylmercury in watersheds upstream from monitoring stations on Indiana streams, 2002–2006.

[km², square kilometer; g/yr, gram per year; µg/m²/yr, microgram per square meter per year; ND, not determined]

Station number	Station name	Upstream drainage area (km²)	Average annual stream load of total mercury (g/yr)	Average annual stream yield[1] of total mercury (µg/m²/yr)	Average annual stream load of methylmercury (g/yr)	Average annual stream yield[1] of methylmercury (µg/m²/yr)
1	Fall Creek near Fortville	447	7,918	17.7	ND	ND
2	Eel River near Logansport	2,043	7,636	3.74	148	0.07
3	Tippecanoe River at Winimac	2,438	1,832	.75	90	.04
4	Wildcat Creek near Lafayette[2]	2,056	37,187	18.1	ND	ND
5	Wabash River at Terre Haute	31,936	65,325	2.05	2,138	.07
6	Mills Creek at Cagles Mill Dam[3]	759	ND	ND	ND	ND
7	White River near Centerton[2]	6,324	250,132	39.6	569	.09
8	White River at Nora	3,149	64,560	20.5	ND	ND
9	Sugar Creek near New Palestine	243	491	2.02	12	.05
10	East Fork Whitewater River near Brookville[3]	986	ND	ND	ND	ND
11	Vernon Fork Muscatatuck River at Vernon	512	6,694	13.1	36	.07
12	East Fork White River at Seymour	6,056	273,693	45.2	ND	ND
13	Blue River at Fredericksburg	732	764	1.04	27	.04
14	Patoka River at Winslow[4]	1,559	9,429	6.05	123	.08
15	White River at Petersburg[5]	28,794	ND	ND	ND	ND

Table 7. Average annual stream loads and yields of unfiltered total mercury and unfiltered methylmercury in watersheds upstream from monitoring stations on Indiana streams, 2002–2006.—Continued

[km², square kilometer; g/yr, gram per year; μg/m²/yr, microgram per square meter per year; ND, not determined]

Station number	Station name	Upstream drainage area (km²)	Average annual stream load of total mercury (g/yr)	Average annual stream yield[1] of total mercury (μg/m²/yr)	Average annual stream load of methylmercury (g/yr)	Average annual stream yield[1] of methylmercury (μg/m²/yr)
16	Busseron Creek near Carlisle	591	2,780	4.70	73	.12
17	Mississinewa River near Peoria[3]	2,093	ND	ND	ND	ND
18	Wabash River near Huntington[3]	1,985	ND	ND	ND	ND
19	Maumee River at New Haven	5,077	27,510	5.42	419	.08
20	Fish Creek near Artic	248	372	1.50	ND	ND
21	St. Joseph River at Elkhart	8,756	6,354	.73	ND	ND
22	Trail Creek at Michigan City[6]	152	ND	ND	ND	ND
23	Deep River at Lake George at Hobart	321	503	1.57	10	.03
24	Kankakee River at Shelby	4,597	6,017	1.31	ND	ND
25	Wabash River at Vincennes[5]	35,628	ND	ND	ND	ND
26	Wabash River at Mt. Carmel, Ill.[7]	74,293	ND	ND	ND	ND

[1] Stream load values were normalized by dividing the stream load, in grams, by the upstream drainage area, in square kilometers.

[2] High uncertainty in unfiltered total mercury or unfiltered methylmercury load; see appendix table 1–4.

[3] Station located downstream from dam; loads were not calculated because of stream-stage control.

[4] Loads in 2006 were not included because of insufficient streamflow data.

[5] Data collected 2004–2006; loads were not calculated because of insufficient concentration data.

[6] Loads were not calculated because of streamflow stagnation and reversal.

[7] Data collected 2002–2004; loads were not calculated because of insufficient concentration data.

Mercury in Fish

Mercury concentrations reported in fish-tissue samples were assumed to be nearly all methylmercury (U.S. Environmental Protection Agency, 1999, 2009; Harris, Krabbenhoft, and others, 2007), and hereinafter are called "mercury concentrations" when referring to fish tissue. Comparisons of mercury concentrations in different types of fish-tissue samples with different fractions of moisture and solids were improved by converting the wet-weight concentrations to dry-weight concentrations. Fish-tissue samples were analyzed for percent total solids, and wet-weight mercury concentrations were multiplied by the reciprocal of the total solids fraction to get dry-weight mercury concentrations.[18] (These dry-weight mercury concentrations are not appropriate for comparison with the mercury water-quality criterion.)

Data for mercury concentrations in 2,225 fish-tissue samples from 502 locations statewide, 1993–2004, were compiled for this report. These fish-tissue samples were from 68 species and were collected at 439 sites on rivers and streams[19] and 63 sites on lakes and reservoirs. Wet-weight mercury concentrations from the 2,225 fish-tissue samples had a median of 123 µg/kg and a maximum of 1,070 µg/kg. When compared with the U.S. Environmental Protection Agency (2001) water-quality criterion of 0.3 mg/kg methylmercury in fish tissue (equivalent to 300 micrograms per kilogram, µg/kg, the units used in the following discussion), 11.6 percent of these concentrations exceeded this criterion. Dry-weight mercury concentrations in the 2,225 fish-tissue samples had a median of 549 µg/kg and a maximum of 4,854 µg/kg.

Data for mercury concentrations in the 26 watersheds included 1,731 fish-tissue samples from 417 locations. These samples were from 83 percent of the 502 locations statewide—358 rivers and streams and 59 lakes and reservoirs. The concentrations were evaluated for the unique drainage areas so that the effect of nested watersheds is not present. Watersheds upstream from nine stations include some areas outside the Indiana border (table 1); the areas outside Indiana range from 2 percent of the watershed (station 18) to 57 percent of the watershed (station 21). Data for mercury concentrations in fish-tissue samples for areas of these watersheds outside Indiana were not available for this study. It is likely that any missing data for areas in other states that could change the interpretations from this study would be in two watersheds with the highest fraction of their total area outside Indiana— station 19 with 47 percent in Ohio and Michigan and station 21 with 57 percent in Michigan (table 1).

Wet-weight mercury concentrations in the 1,731 fish-tissue samples had a median of 130 µg/kg and a maximum of 1,070 µg/kg (from a river in watershed 15); 12.4 percent exceeded the U.S. Environmental Protection Agency (2001) methylmercury criterion. Dry-weight mercury concentrations in the 1,731 fish-tissue samples had a median of 571 µg/kg and a maximum of 4,854 µg/kg (from a lake in watershed 15).

Mercury concentrations in all fish-tissue samples from the 26 watersheds (table 8, fig. 2) were highest in

Watershed 1 – Fall Creek near Fortville,
Watershed 15 –White River at Petersburg,
Watershed 25 – Wabash River at Vincennes, and
Watershed 26 – Wabash River at Mount Carmel, Ill.

The percentage of wet-weight mercury concentrations exceeding the water-quality criterion were highest in watershed 1 (30 percent), watershed 25 (30 percent), and watershed 15 (24 percent). The median wet-weight mercury concentrations were highest in watershed 26 (250 µg/kg), watershed 1 (190 µg/kg), and watershed 25 (170 µg/kg). The percentage of samples with dry-weight mercury concentrations exceeding 1,495 µg/kg (the 90th percentile of concentrations in the 26 watersheds) were highest in watershed 1 (30 percent) and watershed 15 (19 percent). The median dry-weight mercury concentrations were highest in watershed 26 (1,164 µg/kg), watershed 1 (825 µg/kg), and watershed 15 (768 µg/kg).

Graphical and statistical examination of mercury concentrations in fish-tissue samples indicated that watersheds 1, 15, 25, and 26 did not differ significantly and that concentrations in watersheds 15 and 26 were the highest. Boxplots of the distributions of the wet-weight and dry-weight mercury concentrations in fish-tissue samples from 21 of the 26 watersheds with more than 4 samples (fig. 13) showed differences among the watersheds that were significant ($p < 0.001$; Kruskal-Wallis test). Wet-weight mercury concentrations in watersheds 15 and 26 and dry-weight mercury concentrations in watershed 15 were significantly higher than those in watersheds 3, 4, 8, 10, and 24 (Tukey's test).

A coarse-scale review of all fish-tissue mercury samples in the 26 watersheds included samples from streams and lakes of different sizes and different distances from the monitoring station at the downstream end of the watershed. A fine-scale review was done with only the fish-tissue samples collected within 5 km upstream from the monitoring stations at the downstream end of the watersheds. Groups of 5 or more fish-tissue samples were identified for 11 stations: 7 were collected from streams and 4 were collected from reservoirs (table 9).

Mercury concentrations in fish-tissue samples collected within 5 km of the downstream end of 11 watersheds were highest near the following monitoring stations (table 9, fig. 2):

Station 1 – Fall Creek near Fortville
Station 7 – White River near Centerton
Station 15 – White River at Petersburg

The percentage of wet-weight mercury concentrations exceeding the water-quality criterion were highest near station 15 (45 percent), station 1 (40 percent), and station 7 (32 percent). The median wet-weight mercury concentrations were highest near station 15 (240 µg/kg), station 7 (198 µg/kg), and station 1 (190 µg/kg). The median dry-weight mercury

---

[18] Dry-weight mercury concentration was computed as the wet-weight mercury concentration multiplied by a conversion factor. The conversion factor is 1 divided by the percent total solids in the sample, multiplied by 100.

[19] The IDEM database distinguishes natural and manmade lakes from flood-control reservoirs; "streams" are first-order headwaters, and "rivers" are all other flowing waters.

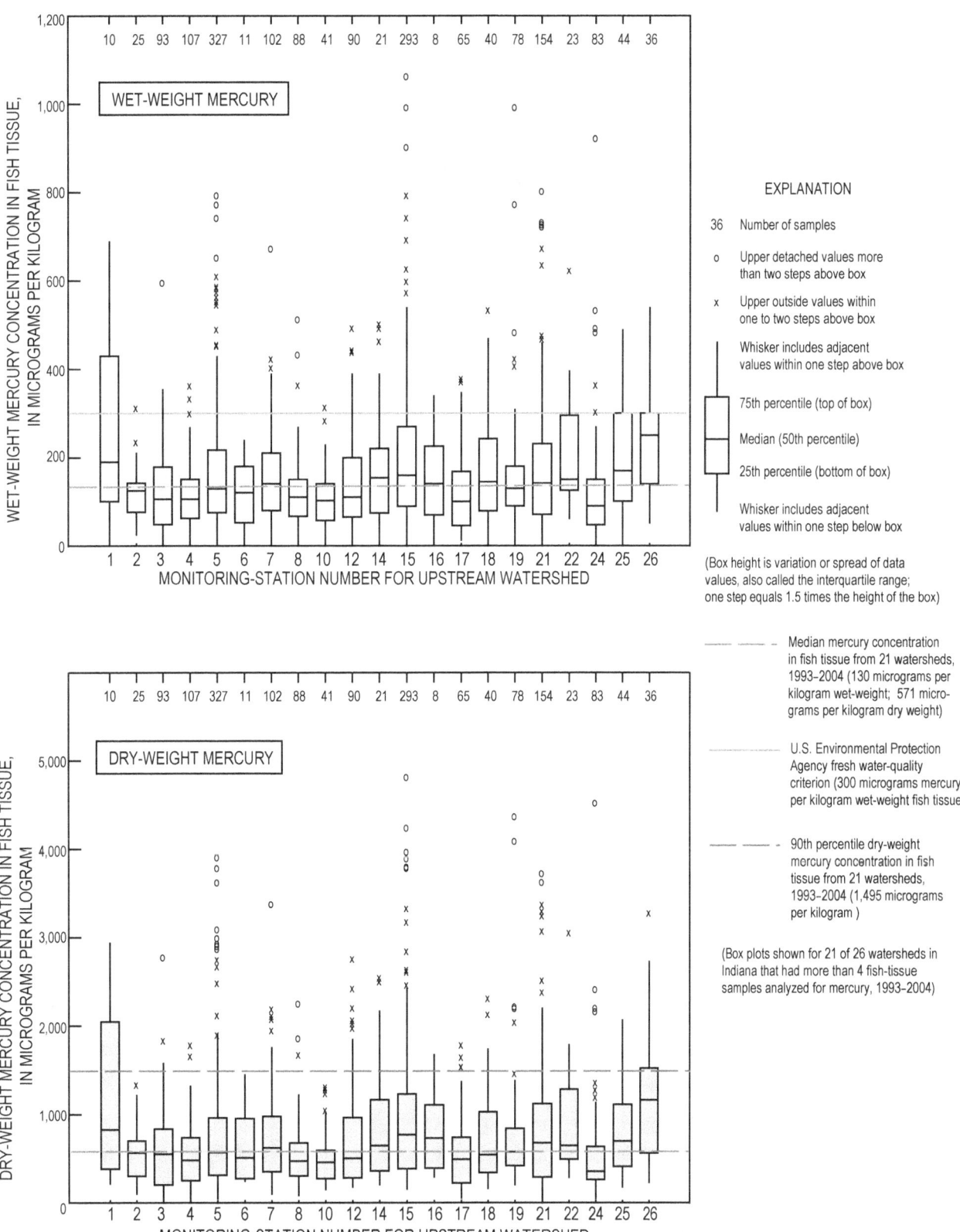

Figure 13. Distributions of wet-weight and dry-weight mercury concentrations in fish-tissue samples from watersheds in Indiana, 1993–2004 (from Indiana Department of Environmental Management Assessment Information Management System).

Table 8. Mercury concentrations in fish-tissue samples from watersheds upstream from monitoring stations on Indiana streams, 1993–2004.

[≥, greater than or equal to; >, greater than; μg/kg, microgram per kilogram; — no data]

Station number	Station name for upstream watershed	Total number of fish tissue samples	Total number of fish-sampling locations	Number of river and stream sampling locations	Number of lake and reservoir sampling locations	Number of wet-weight mercury concentrations ≥criterion[1]	Percentage of wet-weight mercury concentrations ≥criterion[1]	Median wet-weight mercury concentration (μg/kg)	Number of dry-weight mercury concentrations >90th percentile[2]	Percentage of dry-weight mercury concentrations >90th percentile[2]	Median dry-weight mercury concentration (μg/kg)
1	Fall Creek near Fortville	10	3	3	0	3	30	190	3	30	825
2	Eel River near Logansport	25	10	9	1	1	4	124	0	0	565
3	Tippecanoe River at Winimac	93	23	14	9	6	6	105	4	4	548
4	Wildcat Creek near Lafayette	107	18	17	1	3	3	105	2	2	479
5	Wabash River at Terre Haute	327	72	67	5	34	10	129	31	9	568
6	Mills Creek at Cagles Mill Dam	11	3	2	1	0	0	120	0	0	508
7	White River near Centerton	102	24	22	2	13	13	140	10	10	620
8	White River at Nora	88	22	21	1	3	3	110	3	3	471
9	Sugar Creek near New Palestine	0	0	0	0	0	0	—	0	0	—
10	East Fork Whitewater River near Brookville	41	17	14	3	1	2	102	0	0	459
11	Vernon Fork Muscatatuck River at Vernon	4	3	3	0	0	0	—	0	0	—
12	East Fork White River at Seymour	90	31	30	1	11	12	110	11	12	504
13	Blue River at Fredericksburg	4	3	3	0	0	0	—	0	0	NA
14	Patoka River at Winslow	21	10	8	2	4	19	154	4	19	645
15	White River at Petersburg	280	78	66	12	67	24	160	53	19	768
16	Busseron Creek near Carlisle	8	2	1	1	1	13	140	1	13	729

Table 8. Mercury concentrations in fish-tissue samples from watersheds upstream from monitoring stations on Indiana streams, 1993–2004.—Continued

[≥, greater than or equal to; >, greater than; µg/kg, microgram per kilogram; — no data]

Station number	Station name for upstream watershed	Total number of fish tissue samples	Total number of fish-sampling locations	Number of river and stream sampling locations	Number of lake and reservoir sampling locations	Number of wet-weight mercury-concentrations ≥criterion[1]	Percentage of wet-weight mercury concentrations ≥ criterion[1]	Median wet-weight mercury concentration (µg/kg)	Number of dry-weight mercury concentrations >90th percentile[2]	Percentage of dry-weight mercury concentrations >90th percentile[2]	Median dry-weight mercury concentration (µg/kg)
17	Mississinewa River near Peoria	65	20	20	0	5	8	100	4	6	491
18	Wabash River near Huntington	40	10	7	3	5	13	144	5	13	54
19	Maumee River at New Haven	78	16	16	0	8	10	129	6	8	575
20	Fish Creek near Artic	1	1	1	1	0	0	—	0	0	—
21	St. Joseph River at Elkhart	154	8	8	0	19	12	142	17	11	676
22	Trail Creek at Michigan City	23	3	3	0	5	22	150	4	17	644
23	Deep River at Lake George at Hobart	1	1	1	0	0	0	—	0	0	—
24	Kankakee River at Shelby	83	28	17	11	6	7	90	4	5	355
25	Wabash River at Vincennes	44	6	5	1	13	30	170	7	16	696
26	Wabash River at Mt. Carmel, Ill.	36	4	0	4	6	17	250	6	17	1,164

[1]Criterion is U.S. Environmental Protection Agency (2001) water-quality criterion of 300 µg/kg methylmercury in fish tissue. Percentage greater than criterion was computed by dividing the number of concentrations in a watershed that were greater than or equal to 300 µg/kg by the number of samples in the watershed.

[2]The 90th percentile of dry-weight total mercury concentrations is 1,495 µg/kg, in 1,731 samples in Indiana, 1993–2004. Percentage greater than the 90th percentile was computed by dividing the number of concentrations in a watershed that were greater than 1,495 µg/kg by the number of samples in the watershed.

Table 9. Mercury concentrations in fish-tissue samples near monitoring stations on Indiana streams, 1993–2004.

[km, kilometer; μg/kg, microgram per kilogram; ng/L, nanogram per liter; —, no data]

Station number	Station name	Number of fish-tissue samples within 5 km upstream	Number of wet-weight mercury concentrations > criterion[1]	Percentage of wet-weight mercury concentrations > criterion[1]	Median wet-weight mercury concentration (μg/kg)	Number of dry-weight mercury concentrations >90th percentile[2]	Percentage of dry-weight mercury concentrations >90th percentile[2]	Median dry-weight mercury concentration (μg/kg)	Number of uncensored methyl-mercury concentrations	Median methyl-mercury concentration (ng/L)	Median percentage methyl-mercury
					Stream locations						
1	Fall Creek near Fortville	5	2	40	190	2	40	841	8	0.11	4.4
5	Wabash River at Terre Haute	21	6	29	190	4	19	769	14	.15	3.8
7	White River near Centerton	22	7	32	198	5	23	930	15	.15	2.2
15	White River at Petersburg	11	5	45	240	2	18	1,020	9	.20	2.7
19	Maumee River at New Haven	23	5	22	170	4	17	734	13	.25	2.6
22	Trail Creek at Michigan City	23	5	22	150	4	17	644	8	.07	5.0
25	Wabash River at Vincennes	6	0	0	135	0	0	550	9	.16	2.3
					Reservoir locations						
6	Mills Creek at Cagles Mill Dam	9	0	0	149	0	0	663	8	.16	16.1
10	East Fork Whitewater River near Brookville	10	1	10	140	0	0	683	1	—	—
17	Mississinewa River near Peoria	6	0	0	93	0	0	477	11	.09	2.9
18	Wabash River near Huntington	5	0	0	65	0	0	301	14	.13	2.7

[1]Criterion is U.S. Environmental Protection Agency (2001) water-quality criterion of 300 μg/kg methylmercury in fish tissue. Percentage greater than criterion was computed by dividing the number of concentrations that were greater than 300 μg/kg by the number of samples within 5 km of the monitoring station.

[2]The 90th percentile of dry-weight total mercury concentrations is 1,495 μg/kg, in 1,731 samples in Indiana, 1993–2004. Percentage greater than the 90th percentile was computed by dividing the number of concentrations that were greater than 1,495 μg/kg by the number of samples within 5 km of the monitoring station.

concentrations were highest near station 15 (1,020 µg/kg), station 7 (930 µg/kg), and station 1 (841 µg/kg). Consistent with this fine-scale analysis, mercury also was highest in fish from watersheds 1 and 15, based on the coarse-scale analysis.

Mercury concentrations in fish-tissue samples and unfiltered methylmercury concentrations in water samples from nearby monitoring stations did not indicate a consistent relation (table 9). Statistical examination of mercury concentrations in fish-tissue samples collected within 5 km of the downstream end of 11 watersheds indicated that stations 1, 7, and 15 did not differ significantly, although differences among the 11 stations were significant ($p < 0.001$; Kruskal-Wallis test). Wet-weight mercury concentrations near stations 7 and 15 were significantly higher than those near stations 10 and 17 (Tukey's test). Statistical examination of methylmercury concentrations in water samples at these 11 monitoring stations indicated that stations 1, 7, and 15 did not differ significantly, although differences among the 11 stations were significant ($p < 0.001$; Kruskal-Wallis test). Unfiltered methylmercury concentrations in water from stations 7 and 15 were significantly higher than those from station 10 (Tukey's test).

Chasar and others (2009) reported that mercury levels in fish were related to methylmercury concentrations in water, regardless of the trophic level of the fish. The fish-tissue data available for this study were not designed to correspond with the stream mercury- and methylmercury-concentration data. In large watersheds, some of the fish-sampling sites are distant from the stream-monitoring station—as much as 150 km in watershed 15 and 225 km in watershed 25 (fig. 2). The number of fish-tissue samples and the dates of collection vary considerably among the watersheds. Coordination of the fish-tissue sampling sites and schedules with the stream-monitoring network has the potential to reduce these limitations.

Sources of Mercury

The mercury concentrations in stream samples, stream mercury loads, and mercury concentrations in fish-tissue samples from Indiana watersheds, 2002–2006, were influenced by sources of mercury in several ways.

- Atmospheric mercury deposition is a nonpoint source that contributes mercury to a watershed.

- Local stationary sources of mercury emissions in a watershed and their combined annual emissions potentially contribute atmospheric mercury deposition to that watershed. (Regional, continental, and global sources of atmospheric mercury also contribute deposition to a watershed.)

- Mercury in wastewater discharges from permitted outfalls are point sources that potentially contribute mercury to a watershed. (Monitoring data show that mercury was reported in most of the samples of wastewater effluent collected in Indiana.)

- Land cover can affect the rate at which mercury is retained, transformed, and transported to streams in a watershed.

Atmospheric Mercury Deposition

This section of the report summarizes monitoring data for atmospheric mercury wet-deposition rates in Indiana, discusses atmospheric mercury wet- and dry-deposition loading to watersheds, and compares stream mercury yields to the atmospheric-deposition loading rates. In addition, estimates of atmospheric mercury dry-deposition rates are presented, including loads to watersheds and comparisons with atmospheric wet deposition.

As described in the "Mercury Load Calculations" section of this report, average annual atmospheric mercury wet-deposition rates for 2001–2006 were computed with average annual mercury concentrations in precipitation from 9 MDN stations and average annual precipitation from 151 NWS sites in Indiana and 4 surrounding states. The spatial distribution of average annual mercury wet- deposition rates in the study area were interpreted in an isopleth map (fig. 14). The boundaries of the 26 watersheds in this report, including the parts of 6 watersheds outside Indiana, were superimposed on this map.

Average annual mercury wet-deposition rates in the study area ranged from a low of 9 to 10 µg/m²/yr in northern Indiana, which includes isolated areas with less than 9 µg/m²/yr, to a high of 15 to 16 µg/m²/yr in at least six counties in southeastern Indiana (fig. 14), which includes two counties with 15 to 19 µg/m²/yr. The area in southeastern Indiana with the high mercury deposition rate well exceeds the 12-µg/m²/yr average annual mercury wet-deposition rate for five MDN stations in Indiana, 2001–2006 (Risch, 2009).

Some uncertainty exists as to whether the area in southeastern Indiana with the high mercury deposition rate extends further to southwestern Indiana, for two reasons. First, the MDN does not include a station in southwestern Indiana, southeastern Illinois, or northwestern Kentucky that would be sufficiently close to resolve the average annual mercury concentrations in precipitation in southwestern Indiana to a degree that is comparable to other parts of Indiana (fig. 3). In contrast, the number of NWS stations in southwestern Indiana does resolve the average annual precipitation to a degree that is comparable to other parts of Indiana (fig. 3). Second, a substantial number of stationary sources with high annual mercury emissions are in southwestern Indiana (Indiana Department of Environmental Management RAPIDS data for 2002 and 2005), which could contribute to higher mercury concentrations in precipitation. Uncertainty about the boundaries of the area in southern Indiana with a high mercury wet-deposition rate also was reported in an analysis of 2004–2005 data by Risch and Fowler (2008).

Average annual atmospheric mercury wet-deposition loads, in grams per year, were computed for each watershed with data from the isopleth map (fig. 14) by using the method

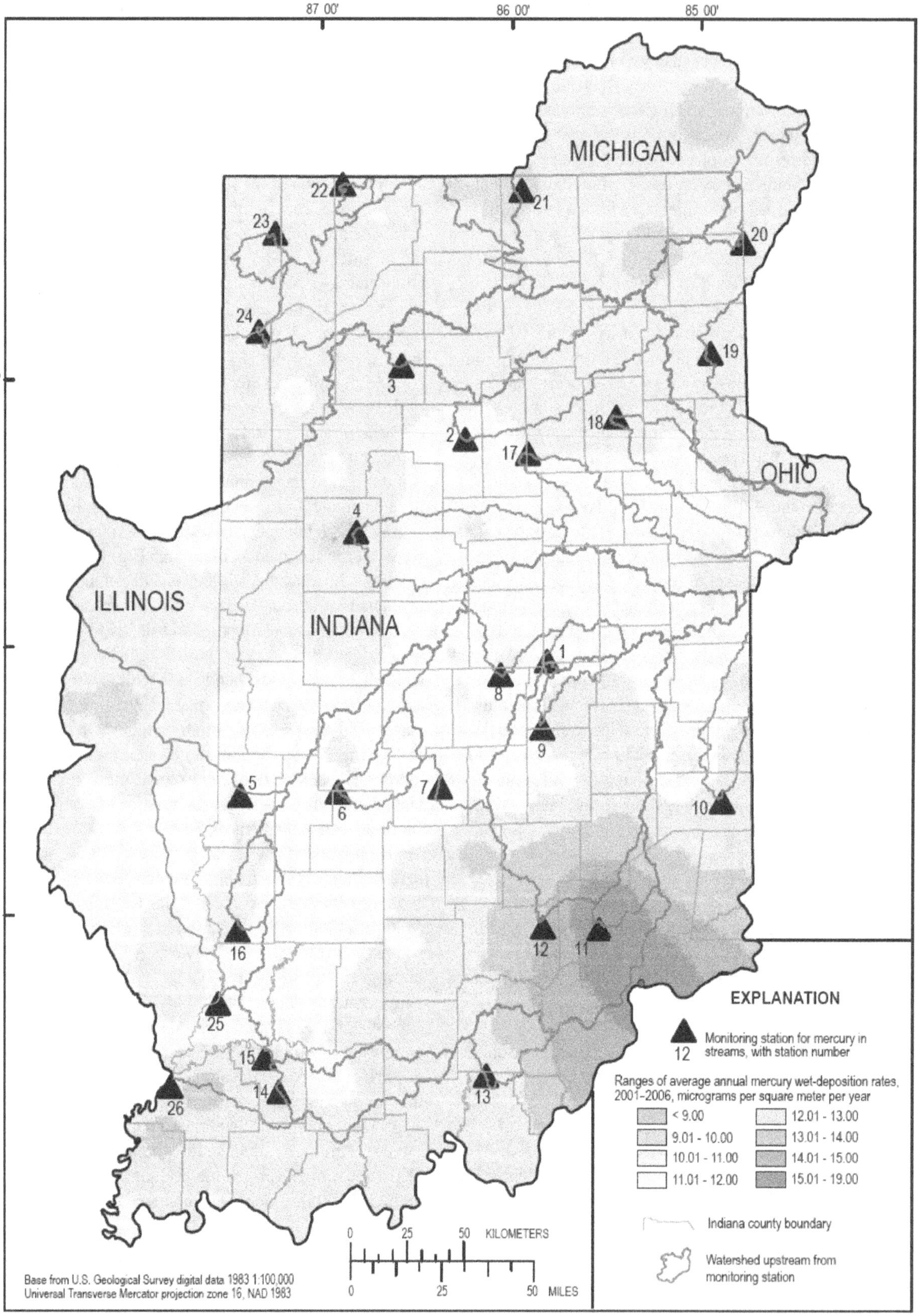

Figure 14.   Isopleth map of average annual mercury wet-deposition rates, 2001–2006, showing upstream watershed boundaries for monitoring stations on Indiana streams.

described in the "Mercury Load Calculations" section of the report. The average annual atmospheric mercury loadings entering the watersheds (also called loading rates), in micrograms per square meter per year, were computed by dividing the loads by the watershed upstream drainage areas.

Atmospheric mercury loading rates for Indiana watersheds, 2001–2006, ranged from 9.60 to 14.8 $\mu g/m^2/yr$, with a median of 11.3 $\mu g/m^2/yr$ (table 10). Watershed 11, which had the highest atmospheric mercury loading rate, 14.8 $\mu g/m^2/yr$, is in the area in southeastern Indiana with the high mercury wet-deposition rate (fig. 14). Watersheds 12, 13, 14, and 15 in southern Indiana (fig. 14) had atmospheric mercury loading rates higher than the 12 $\mu g/m^2$ average for five MDN stations in Indiana, 2001–2006 (Risch, 2009).

The average annual stream yields of total mercury were positively correlated with the average annual atmospheric mercury wet-deposition loading rates in 18 watersheds for which yield and loading rates were available (Kendall's tau[20] = 0.47; p = 0.007). Stream mercury yields were not related uniformly to atmospheric mercury loadings. The percentage of stream mercury yield from atmospheric mercury wet-deposition loading ranged from 7 percent at station 3 to 360 percent at station 12 (table 10, fig. 15). Stream mercury yields from 13 of the 18 watersheds were less than 100 percent of the atmospheric loading, indicating that some of the atmospheric mercury entering the watersheds was not delivered by the stream. Rather, this mercury was retained in the watershed or re-emitted to the air.

Other investigators reported that much of atmospheric mercury wet deposition apparently is retained in the watershed before reaching the stream, a finding that is consistent with this observation in Indiana. Shanley and others (2008) used MDN data and stream-monitoring data for five watersheds to observe that 60 to 97 percent of the mercury wet deposition was retained. Brigham and others (2009) used MDN data and stream-monitoring data for eight watersheds and observed that stream mercury loads were less than 50 percent of atmospheric mercury loads. Hintelmann and others (2002) used an experimental approach to monitor the fate of atmospheric mercury in wet deposition. They found that much of the mercury was retained in vegetation and soils in a boreal forest study site, and the mercury levels in runoff responded slowly to changes in mercury deposition rates.

A ratio of mercury yield to mercury loading less than 100 percent also may involve inputs other than atmospheric deposition. Mason and Sullivan (1998) studied mercury transport in an urbanized watershed and observed stream mercury yields that were 60 to 80 percent of atmospheric wet-deposition

loads, concluding that sources other than regional atmospheric deposition were contributing some of the mercury load to the stream.

Atmospheric mercury dry deposition was not measured directly in Indiana during 2001–2006. Other investigators have reported that atmospheric mercury dry deposition can be a substantial portion of the total atmospheric mercury deposition. Depending on location, modeled predictions and inferential estimates of atmospheric mercury dry-deposition rates can be equal to, or several times, the atmospheric mercury wet-deposition rates (Cohen and others, 2004; Poissant and others, 2004; Seigneur and others, 2004; Miller and others, 2005; Lyman and others, 2007).

Atmospheric mercury dry-deposition rates in Indiana were estimated for this report. These estimates are not based on a dataset as extensive as that for wet deposition in Indiana. In 2004, air samples were collected every six days at three MDN stations in Indiana (IN20, IN21, and IN26; fig. 2) by means of manual methods described in Risch and others (2007). Concentrations of three atmospheric mercury fractions or "species"— reactive gaseous mercury (RGM), particulate-bound mercury (PHg), and gaseous elemental mercury (GEM)—were determined in these air samples with low-level methods. Dry-deposition rates for the three mercury species were estimated with the inferential method described by Seigneur and others (2004), Miller and others (2005), and Lyman and others (2007). Annual dry-deposition rates for each species (table 11), in micrograms per square meter per year, were computed in a series of steps. Seasonal median daily concentrations of RGM, PHg, and GEM in samples from the Indiana stations, reported in Risch and others (2007), were multiplied by a representative vertical deposition velocity for each species reported in the scientific literature (summarized in Seigneur and others, 2004). The resulting daily dry-deposition rates were multiplied by the number of days for each season—winter/fall (180 days), spring (90 days), and summer (90 days) to get seasonal dry-deposition rates. Annual dry-deposition rates for each species were the sum of the three seasonal rates.

The annual dry-deposition rates for each mercury species (table 11) were multiplied by the upstream drainage area of each watershed to determine the atmospheric mercury dry-deposition loading rate for each watershed. The vertical deposition velocity for GEM in forest land cover is higher than that in nonforest land cover, and the GEM dry-deposition rate in forest land cover is 6 times higher (table 11). The reason for the higher dry-deposition rate is that forest canopies are sinks for GEM (Grigal, 2002). Therefore, the GEM dry-deposition rate in forest land cover was applied to the upstream drainage area in forest cover in each watershed, and the GEM dry-deposition rate in nonforest land cover was applied to the remaining upstream drainage area in the watershed (table 12). Data for forest land cover was from the NLCD (Multi-Resolution Land Characteristics Consortium, 2001), as described in the "Sources of Data" section of this report. Further discussion is in the "Land Cover" section later in this report.

---

[20] The Kendall's tau correlation coefficient (Helsel and Hirsch, 1995) is a nonparametric, rank-based procedure to evaluate the relation between two variables. A strong positive correlation is indicated by a Kendall's tau of 0.70 or higher. In this report, a moderate positive correlation is indicated by a Kendall's tau higher than 0.35 and less than 0.70. A significance level (α) of 0.05 or less was used to accept a statistically significant difference. The p-value is the significance attained by the data. The smaller the p-value, the more believable the statistical difference.

Table 10.   Average annual atmospheric mercury wet-deposition loads and loading rates, 2001–2006, and average annual stream yields of total mercury, 2002–2006, in watersheds upstream from monitoring stations on Indiana streams

[g, gram; km², square kilometer; µg/m²/yr, microgram per square meter per year; ND, not determined]

Station number	Station name	Average annual atmospheric mercury wet-deposition load (g)	Upstream drainage area (km²)	Average annual atmospheric mercury wet-deposition loading rate (µg/m²/yr)	Average annual stream mercury yield (µg/m²/yr)	Ratio of stream mercury yield to wet atmospheric mercury loading (percent)
1	Fall Creek near Fortville	5,278	447	11.8	17.7	150
2	Eel River near Logansport	21,831	2,043	10.7	3.74	35
3	Tippecanoe River at Winimac	26,044	2,438	10.7	.75	7
4	Wildcat Creek near Lafayette	23,409	2,056	11.4	18.1	159
5	Wabash River at Terre Haute	348,329	31,936	10.9	2.05	19
6	Mills Creek at Cagles Mill Dam	8,856	759	11.7	ND	ND
7	White River near Centerton	72,051	6,324	11.4	39.6	347
8	White River at Nora	35,634	3,149	11.3	20.5	181
9	Sugar Creek near New Palestine	2,724	243	11.2	2.02	18
10	East Fork Whitewater River near Brookville	11,820	986	12.0	ND	ND
11	Vernon Fork Muscatatuck River at Vernon	7,571	512	14.8	13.1	88
12	East Fork White River at Seymour	76,042	6,056	12.6	45.2	360
13	Blue River at Fredericksburg	9,422	732	12.9	1.04	8
14	Patoka River at Winslow	19,168	1,559	12.3	6.05	49
15	White River at Petersburg	352,794	28,794	12.23	ND	ND
16	Busseron Creek near Carlisle	6,505	591	11.0	4.70	43
17	Mississinewa River near Peoria	23,774	2,093	11.4	ND	ND
18	Wabash River near Huntington	21,517	1,985	10.8	ND	ND
19	Maumee River at New Haven	52,580	5,077	10.4	5.42	52
20	Fish Creek near Artic	2,516	248	10.1	1.50	15
21	St. Joseph River at Elkhart	89,035	8,756	10.2	.73	7
22	Trail Creek at Michigan City	1,457	152	9.60	ND	ND

Table 10. Average annual atmospheric mercury wet-deposition loads and loading rates, 2001–2006, and average annual stream yields of total mercury, 2002–2006, in watersheds upstream from monitoring stations on Indiana streams.—Continued

[g, gram; km², square kilometer; µg/m²/yr, microgram per square meter per year; ND, not determined]

Station number	Station name	Average annual atmospheric mercury wet-deposition load (g)	Upstream drainage area (km²)	Average annual atmospheric mercury wet-deposition loading rate (µg/m²/yr)	Average annual stream mercury yield (µg/m²/yr)	Ratio of stream mercury yield to wet atmospheric mercury loading (percent)
23	Deep River at Lake George at Hobart	3,494	321	10.9	1.57	14
24	Kankakee River at Shelby	48,416	4,597	10.5	1.31	12
25	Wabash River at Vincennes	388,993	35,628	10.9	ND	ND
26	Wabash River at Mt. Carmel, Ill.	852,659	74,293	11.5	ND	ND

Table 11. Atmospheric mercury species concentrations, vertical deposition velocities, and annual dry-deposition rates in Indiana, 2004.

[cm/s, centimeter per second; pg/m³, picogram per cubic meter; µg/m²/yr, microgram per square meter per year]

Atmospheric mercury species	Vertical deposition velocity[1] (cm/s)	Winter/Fall		Spring		Summer		Annual dry deposition rate[5] (µg/m²/yr)
		Median daily concentration[2] (pg/m³)	Seasonal dry deposition rate[3] (µg/m²)	Median daily cocentration (pg/m³)	Seasonal dry deposition rate[4] (µg/m²)	Median daily concentration (pg/m³)	Seasonal dry deposition rate[4] (µg/m²)	
Reactive gaseous	0.50	2.90	0.225	1.50	0.058	0.80	0.033	0.317
Particulate bound	.10	3.70	.057	5.95	.046	4.10	.034	.137
Gaseous elemental (land)	.01	1,480	2.30	1,320	1.03	1,340	1.10	4.43
Gaseous elemental (forest)	.06	1,480	13.8	1,320	6.16	1,340	6.60	26.6

[1] From Seigneur and others (2004).

[2] From Risch and others (2007).

[3] Seasonal dry deposition rate computed as the product of the vertical deposition velocity and median daily concentration. Units were converted to µg/m²/day and multiplied by 180 days.

[4] Seasonal dry deposition rate computed as the product of the vertical deposition velocity and median daily concentration. Units were converted to µg/m²/day and multiplied by 90 days.

[5] Annual dry deposition rate computed as the sum of the three seasonal dry deposition rates.

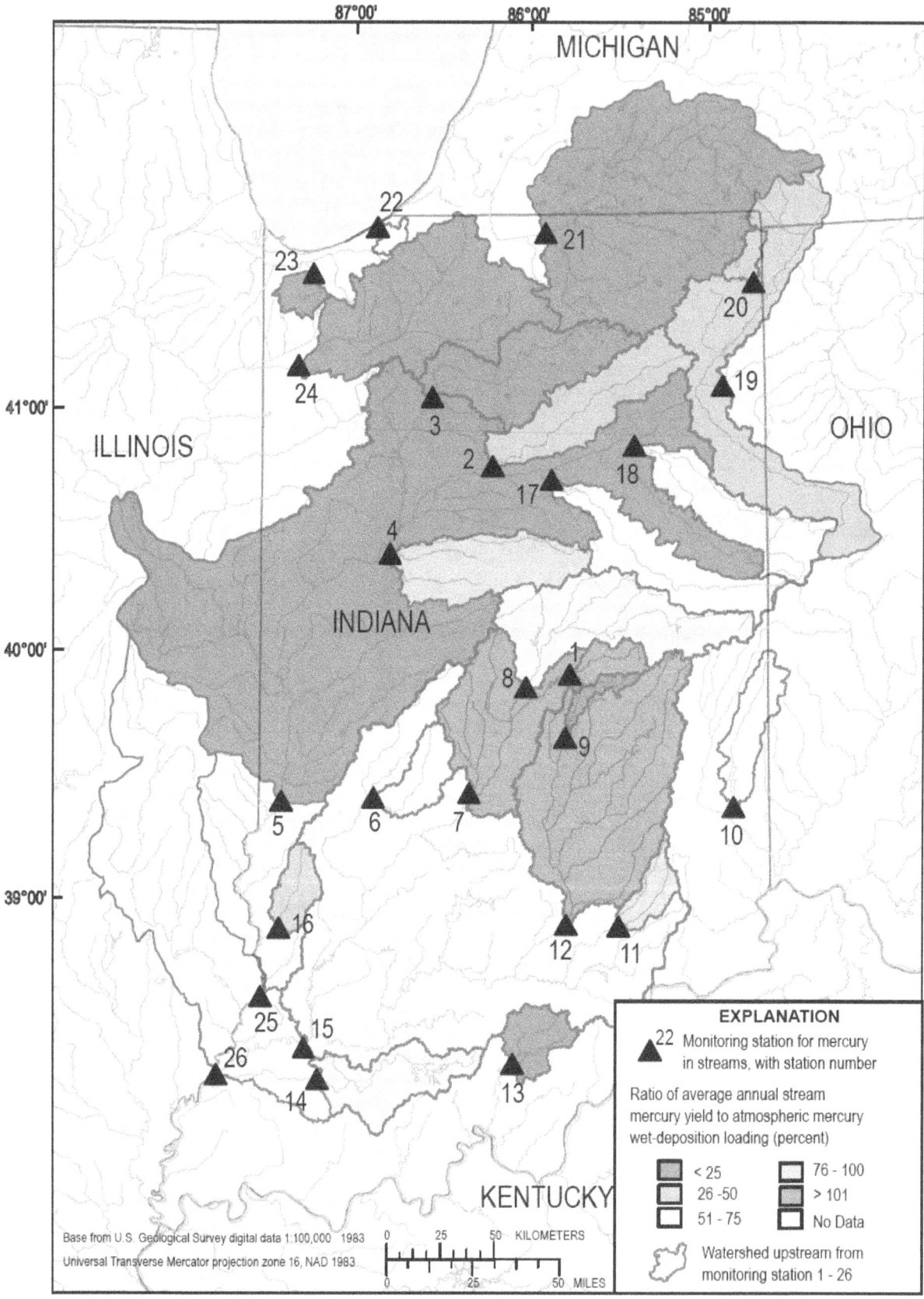

Figure 15.   Ratios of average annual stream mercury yield to atmospheric mercury wet -deposition loading in watersheds upstream from monitoring stations on Indiana streams, 2001–2006.

Annual atmospheric mercury dry-deposition loading rates to the watersheds ranged from 5.6 $\mu g/m^2/yr$ (watershed 4) to 13.6 $\mu g/m^2/yr$ (watershed 14). The median rate was 7.2 $\mu g/m^2/yr$. The atmospheric mercury dry-deposition loading rates to the watersheds were 0.49 to 1.4 times the atmospheric mercury wet-deposition loading rates.

Watersheds 7 and 12 had stream mercury yields that were 224 and 233 percent, respectively, of the combined atmospheric mercury wet and dry loadings (table 12). Other mercury inputs besides atmospheric deposition apparently contributed approximately half of the stream mercury yields in watersheds 7 and 12. The stream mercury yields were 3.9 to 120 percent of the combined atmospheric mercury wet and dry loading in 16 of 18 watersheds (table 12).

Ratios of stream mercury yields to the combined atmospheric mercury wet- and dry-deposition loading rates, combined with knowledge from other investigators, indicate that three conditions may be present in Indiana: (1) Uncommonly, watersheds have stream mercury yields higher than the combined atmospheric mercury wet and dry loading rates and receive mercury input from sources other than atmospheric deposition. One of these other sources is mercury in wastewater discharges, discussed in a following section of this report. Another source is mercury from atmospheric deposition that was retained on soil in the watershed until that soil was eroded and washed into streams. Typically, watersheds have stream mercury yields less than the combined atmospheric mercury wet and dry loading rates and either receive (2) mercury input entirely from atmospheric deposition, with the excess loading retained in the watershed or re-emitted to the air, or (3) mercury input from atmospheric deposition and other sources, with excess loading retained in the watershed or re-emitted to the air.

Mercury Emissions to the Atmosphere

Mercury emissions to the atmosphere were examined for their potential influence on total mercury concentrations and stream yields of total mercury in the watersheds. Locations of stationary sources of mercury emissions to the atmosphere (fig. 6) and their annual mercury emissions in 2002 and 2005 were obtained from the RAPIDS data for Indiana (Indiana Department of Environmental Management, Office of Air Quality, written commun., 2005, 2008). The number of mercury-emission sources and the annual emissions in 2002 and 2005 were totaled for each watershed (appendix table 1–5).

In 2002, 128 stationary sources in the 26 watersheds emitted 2,830 kg (6,289 lb) of mercury. The highest emissions and highest number of stationary sources were 1,097 kg (2,438 lb) of mercury from 25 sources in watershed 5 and 617 kg (1,371 lb) of mercury from 20 sources in watershed 15. In watersheds 2, 7, 19, and 24, annual emissions in 2002 were greater than 150 kg.

In 2005, 99 stationary sources in the 26 watersheds emitted 1,906 kg (4,236 lb of mercury). Similar to 2002, the highest emissions in 2005 were 376 kg (836 lb) of mercury from 22 sources in watershed 5 and 586 kg (1,302 lb) of mercury from 18 sources in watershed 15. Annual emissions were greater than 150 kg in watersheds 7, 19, and 24.

For the 26 watersheds in Indiana, there were positive correlations between the average total mercury concentrations in water and four variables: the number of emission sources in the watersheds in 2002 and 2005 and the annual mercury emissions in 2002 and 2005.[21] Even so, a consistent relation was not observed, and atmospheric mercury transport and source-area modeling for the watersheds was beyond the scope of this report.

A number of factors determine how much, if any, of the mercury emitted within a watershed will contribute to the mercury concentrations and stream mercury yield at the downstream end of that watershed. These factors include the location of an emission source in the watershed, prevailing wind direction, precipitation conditions, height above ground for the emissions from the stationary source, and type of mercury species in the emissions.

The influence of local and regional sources on atmospheric mercury deposition has been reported by other investigators. Using a model to trace atmospheric mercury wet and dry deposition to emissions sources, the U.S. Environmental Protection Agency (2008) found that areas of high deposition frequently were dominated by one or more nearby sources and by collective sources within a state. For a location of high deposition in Indiana, their model calculated that 54 percent of the deposition came from local sources in the state. Seigneur and others (2006) used different models to predict atmospheric mercury wet and dry deposition in the vicinity of powerplants. The models calculated that 9 to 53 percent of the mercury emitted by typical powerplants fell within 9.3 km; 1 to 8 percent fell within 50 km. Keeler and others (2006) applied two multivariate statistical models and meteorological analysis to monitoring data collected in 2003–2004 at a site in the Ohio River valley of eastern Ohio. They found that the majority of the mercury wet deposition was contributed by coal combustion from local and regional sources. Cohen and others (2004) used a sophisticated source-receptor model to estimate mercury wet and dry deposition to the Great Lakes. For Lake Michigan, as an example, they found that approximately half the deposition came from local sources within 100 km of the lake and that the largest contribution was from coal combustion.

Continued monitoring of atmospheric mercury wet deposition in Indiana provides a dataset for modeling the contribution of local and regional sources to stream mercury yields from watersheds. However, long-term monitoring data for

---

[21] The moderate positive correlation of average unfiltered total mercury concentration to the following factors is based on the Kendall's tau statistics and p-values listed ($\alpha = 0.05$): 2002 mercury emissions (tau = 0.35, p = 0.013); 2002 emissions sources (tau = 0.40, p = 0.004); 2005 mercury emissions (tau = 0.35, p = 0.010); and 2005 mercury sources (tau = 0 35, p = 0.010).

Table 12. Annual atmospheric mercury dry-deposition and wet-deposition loading rates and annual stream yields of total mercury in watersheds upstream from monitoring stations on Indiana streams

[km², square kilometer; µg/m²/yr, microgram per square meter per year; ND, not determined]

Station number	Station name	Upstream drainage area with forest land cover (km²)	Upstream drainage area with non-forest land cover (km²)	Annual atmospheric mercury dry-deposition loading rate (µg/m²/yr)	Average annual atmospheric mercury wet-deposition loading rate (µg/m²/yr)	Combined atmospheric mercury wet and dry loading (µg/m²/yr)	Average annual stream mercury yield (µg/m²/yr)	Ratio of stream mercury yield to combined atmospheric mercury wet and dry loading (percent)
1	Fall Creek near Fortville	24	423	6.1	11.8	17.9	17.7	99
2	Eel River near Logansport	169	1,874	6.7	10.7	17.4	3.74	21
3	Tippecanoe River at Winimac	217	2,221	6.9	10.7	17.5	0.75	4.3
4	Wildcat Creek near Lafayette	64	1,992	5.6	11.4	17.0	18.1	107
5	Wabash River at Terre Haute	2,757	29,179	6.8	10.9	17.7	2.05	12
6	Mills Creek at Cagles Mill Dam	116	643	8.3	11.7	19.9	ND	ND
7	White River near Centerton	396	5,928	6.3	11.4	17.7	39.6	224
8	White River at Nora	128	3,021	5.8	11.3	17.1	20.5	120
9	Sugar Creek near New Palestine	12	231	6.0	11.2	17.2	2.02	12
10	East Fork Whitewater River near Brookville	171	815	8.7	12.0	20.7	ND	ND
11	Vernon Fork Muscatatuck River at Vernon	176	336	12.5	14.8	27.3	13.1	48
12	East Fork White River at Seymour	530	5,526	6.8	12.6	19.4	45.2	233
13	Blue River at Fredericksburg	202	530	11.0	12.9	23.9	1.04	4.4
14	Patoka River at Winslow	613	946	13.6	12.3	25.9	6.05	23

Table 12. Annual atmospheric mercury dry-deposition and wet-deposition loading rates and annual stream yields of total mercury in watersheds upstream from monitoring stations on Indiana streams.—Continued

[km², square kilometer; µg/m²/yr, microgram per square meter per year; ND, not determined]

Station number	Station name	Upstream drainage area with forest land cover (km²)	Upstream drainage area with non-forest land cover (km²)	Annual atmospheric mercury dry-deposition loading rate (µg/m²/yr)	Average annual atmospheric mercury wet-deposition loading rate (µg/m²/yr)	Combined atmospheric mercury wet and dry loading (µg/m²/yr)	Average annual stream mercury yield (µg/m²/yr)	Ratio of stream mercury yield to combined atmospheric mercury wet and dry loading (percent)
15	White River at Petersburg	6,884	21,910	10.2	12.2	22.4	ND	ND
16	Busseron Creek near Carlisle	150	441	10.5	11.0	21.5	4.70	22
17	Mississinewa River near Peoria	154	1,939	6.5	11.4	17.9	ND	ND
18	Wabash River near Huntington	111	1,874	6.1	10.8	17.0	ND	ND
19	Maumee River at New Haven	506	4,571	7.1	10.4	17.5	5.42	31
20	Fish Creek near Artic	45	203	8.9	10.1	19.1	1.50	7.9
21	St. Joseph River at Elkhart	1,313	7,443	8.2	10.2	18.4	0.73	3.9
22	Trail Creek at Michigan City	58	94	13.3	9.60	22.9	ND	ND
23	Deep River at Lake George at Hobart	58	263	8.9	10.9	19.8	1.57	7.9
24	Kankakee River at Shelby	515	4,082	7.4	10.5	17.9	1.31	7.3
25	Wabash River at Vincennes	3,454	32,174	7.0	10.9	17.4	ND	ND
26	Wabash River at Mt. Carmel, Ill.	11,973	62,320	8.5	11.5	17.5	ND	ND

estimating dry deposition of atmospheric mercury are unavailable for locations in Indiana. The addition of datasets for atmospheric mercury dry deposition in Indiana would improve modeling certainty regarding the sources of stream mercury yields from watersheds; these data should include air-quality mercury, throughfall mercury, and litterfall mercury (Harris, Krabbenhoft, and others, 2007).

Mercury in Wastewater

The potential influence of mercury in wastewater on total mercury concentrations and stream mercury yields in the watersheds was examined by using monitoring data for mercury in wastewater-effluent samples and the number of permitted outfalls in the watersheds. Total mercury was routinely detected in treated wastewater effluent in Indiana, often at concentrations exceeding a water-quality criterion. Although there are thousands of wastewater outfalls and only a small percentage of these outfalls have been analyzed for mercury, the potential was demonstrated for mercury in wastewater to be discharged to Indiana watersheds. In some watersheds, discharges of mercury in wastewater may be contributing to total mercury concentrations in water and stream mercury yields.

Statewide, total mercury concentrations were determined in 534 grab samples of treated wastewater effluent collected by operators of 64 POTWs throughout Indiana. Total mercury concentrations ranged from <0.05 to 88 ng/L, with a median of 2.3 ng/L. Total mercury concentrations were higher than the reporting limit in 96 percent of the effluent samples that were analyzed. Compared to Indiana water-quality criteria for mercury, the 12-ng/L Indiana chronic-aquatic criterion was equaled or exceeded in 10 percent of the samples; the 1.8-ng/L Great Lakes human-health criterion was equaled or exceeded in 60 percent, and the 1.3-ng/L Great Lakes wildlife criterion was equaled or exceeded in 72 percent.

Among the 26 watersheds, total mercury concentrations were reported in 402 grab samples of wastewater effluent from 50 POTWs in 15 watersheds. Concentrations ranged from <0.05 to 88 ng/L, with a median of 2.9 ng/L. Concentrations were higher than the reporting limit in 96 percent of the effluent samples that were analyzed. Compared to Indiana water-quality criteria for mercury, the 12-ng/L Indiana chronic-aquatic criterion was equaled or exceeded in 12 percent of the samples; the 1.8-ng/L Great Lakes human-health criterion was equaled or exceeded in 68 percent, and the 1.3-ng/L Great lakes wildlife criterion was equaled or exceeded in 81 percent. The average mercury concentration in effluent samples was computed for the 50 POTWs (table 13, fig. 16) and for those with 3 or more samples, the values ranged from 0.83 to 22.2 ng/L. The average mercury concentrations in effluent samples equaled or exceeded the 1.3-ng/L Great Lakes wildlife criterion at 45 of the 50 POTWs.

Information from the literature indicates that wastewater may be a source of total mercury in watersheds. The National Association of Clean Water Agencies (NACWA, 2000) reported a 138-ng/L average concentration of mercury in domestic wastewater in different parts of the country with no industrial or commercial inputs. Several common household and toiletry items were found to contain levels of mercury that could account for part of this average, but most of the mercury was attributed to human waste. A laboratory evaluation of mercury removal by amalgam separators used in dentists' offices (Fan and others, 2002) showed 95-percent effectiveness, indicating some mercury in wastewater could be contributed by dentists' offices, even when amalgam separators are in use. The NACWA 2000 report observed that POTWs remove 97 percent of the mercury in their influent, consistent with a removal rate for a POTW studied by Balogh and Liang (1995). A study of the Scioto River near Columbus, Ohio, in 2004 by Lyons and others (2006) reported that the highest mercury concentrations were downstream from two POTWs.

This information demonstrates the potential for mercury in wastewater to be contributing to stream mercury yields in some Indiana watersheds, including three in particular. Watersheds 7 and 19 had high total mercury concentrations in water (table 3). Watersheds 7 and 12 had high stream mercury yields (table 12), and the high ratios of stream mercury yield to atmospheric mercury wet- and dry-deposition load indicated that inputs other than atmospheric mercury deposition were likely. Mercury was reported in samples of treated wastewater effluent in watersheds 7, 12, and 19 (table 13). At a POTW upstream from station 7, the average mercury concentration was 10.9 ng/L in 20 samples. At a POTW upstream from station 12, the average mercury concentration was 11.5 ng/L in 22 samples. One of the highest average effluent concentrations was 22.2 ng/L in 39 samples at a POTW upstream from station 19. These average mercury concentrations in effluent samples were higher than the median total mercury concentrations in water samples at stations 7, 12, and 19 (table 13).

According to the Permit Compliance System database for National Pollutant Discharge Elimination System permits in Indiana in 2005, there were 5,551 permitted outfalls of treated and untreated wastewater. In the watersheds upstream from the 26 monitoring stations on Indiana streams, there were 4,144 permitted outfalls (fig. 7, table 14). Of these, 1,044 (25 percent) were classified as outfalls at a major facility with the capacity to discharge up to 1 Mgal/d. The outfalls are characterized in the permit database as discharging sanitary wastewater, process wastewater, cooling water, storm runoff, and mixtures of these types, along with some mine-pit dewatering.

Total mercury in some watersheds could be attributed to mercury in wastewater because the average total mercury concentrations in water showed a moderate correlation with the number of outfalls (Kendall's tau = 0.47, p = 0.001). Three watersheds with high mercury concentrations in water and high stream mercury yields had a substantial number of outfalls: 401 in watershed 7, 225 in watershed 12, and 182 in watershed 19.

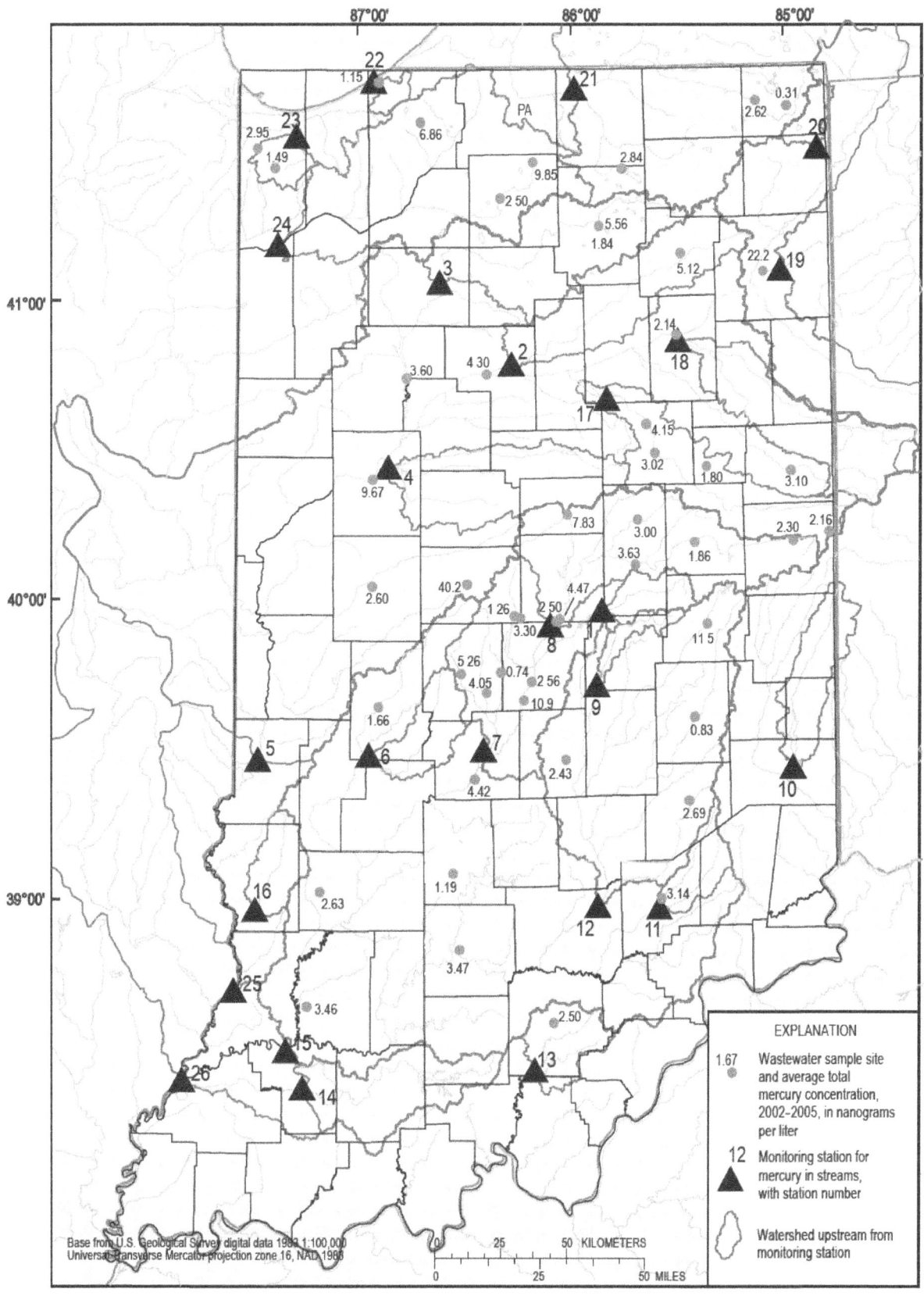

Figure 16.   Treatment works upstream from monitoring stations on Indiana streams, with average total mercury concentrations in samples of wastewater effluent, 2002–2005 (from U.S. Environmental Agency Permit Compliance System).

Although the number of outfalls indicates a potential for discharge of mercury in wastewater, the volume of the waste-water discharge may be important because the average total mercury concentrations in water samples showed a moderate correlation with the number of outfalls at major facilities (Kendall's tau = 0.37, p = 0.008). Three watersheds with high mercury concentrations in water and high stream mercury yields had outfalls at major facilities: 45 percent in watershed 7, 24 percent in watershed 12, and 37 percent in watershed 19 (table 14).

Monitoring of flow volumes and mercury concentrations in wastewater, over a range of flow conditions at permitted outfalls in selected watersheds, would be needed to characterize the relative importance of discharges of mercury in wastewater as compared to atmospheric deposition. The two watersheds with approximately half of the stream mercury yield from sources other than atmospheric deposition (watersheds 7 and 12) might be appropriate locations to start this type of monitoring.

Table 13. Average total mercury concentrations in grab samples of wastewater effluent at treatment works upstream from monitoring stations on Indiana streams, 2002–2005.

[ng/L; nanograms per liter; sample data not available for stations 1, 4, 6, 9, 10, 14, 16, 18, 20, 25, and 26]

Station number	Station name for upstream watershed	Average total mercury concentration in samples[1] (ng/L)	Number of wastewater-effluent samples	Number of censored values
2	Eel River near Logansport	5.12	8	4
3	Tippecanoe River at Winimac	1.84	2	0
		5.56	19	0
5	Wabash River at Terre Haute	2.60	3	0
		2.14	12	1
		9.67	10	0
		4.30	11	1
		3.60	1	0
		3.10	2	0
7	White River near Centerton	3.30	13	0
		5.26	10	0
		.74	1	0
		2.56	9	0
		10.9	20	0
		4.05	8	0
		1.26	6	2
8	White River at Nora	3.00	14	0
		3.63	6	0
		2.50	7	0
		4.47	13	0
		1.86	9	2
		7.83	8	1
		2.30	2	0
11	Vernon Fork Muscatatuck River at Vernon	3.14	7	0
12	East Fork White River at Seymour	2.43	18	0
		2.69	8	0
		11.5	22	0
		.83	4	0

Land Cover

Land cover affects the rate at which mercury is retained, transformed, and transported to streams in a watershed. For this report, land cover was examined graphically, statistically, and with lines of evidence for relations to mercury concentrations in stream samples, stream mercury yields, and mercury in fish-tissue samples. Land-cover classes from the 2001 NLCD (Multi-Resolution Land Characteristics Consortium, 2001) were summarized as described in the "Sources of Data" section. For each of the 26 watersheds upstream from the monitoring stations on Indiana streams, the percentage of the drainage area in each land-cover class was determined (appendix table 1–6). Some land-cover classes were sparsely represented in the watersheds; some classes that were represented were similar. The 20 land-cover classes were combined into 7 land-cover types for discussion in this report:

- Urban: Low-intensity residential, high-intensity residential, and commercial/industrial/transportation.

- Forest: Deciduous forest, evergreen forest, mixed forest, and shrubland.

Table 13. Average total mercury concentrations in grab samples of wastewater effluent at treatment works upstream from monitoring stations on Indiana streams, 2002–2005.—Continued

[ng/L; nanograms per liter; sample data not available for stations 1, 4, 6, 9, 10, 14, 16, 18, 20, 25, and 26]

Station number	Station name for upstream watershed	Average total mercury concentration in samples[1] (ng/L)	Number of wastewater-effluent samples	Number of censored values
13	Blue River at Fredericksburg	2.50	1	0
15	White River at Petersburg	3.47	13	0
		1.19	2	0
		1.66	5	1
		40.2	2	0
		2.63	3	1
		4.42	5	0
		3.46	7	1
17	Mississinewa River near Peoria	3.02	8	0
		1.80	2	0
		4.15	4	0
		2.16	6	1
19	Maumee River at New Haven	22.2	39	0
21	St. Joseph River at Elkhart	.31	2	0
		2.62	3	0
		2.84	8	0
22	Trail Creek at Michigan City	1.15	7	0
23	Deep River at Lake George at Hobart	1.49	1	0
		2.95	14	0
24	Kankakee River at Shelby	9.85	10	0
		6.86	5	0
		2.50	2	0

[1]Average total mercury concentrations that include censored values were computed with the Adjusted Maximum Likelihood Estimate procedure (Helsel, 2005) by using statistical software (S-Plus, Tibco Software, 2008).

Table 14. Number of permitted outfalls in 2005 for watersheds upstream from monitoring stations on Indiana streams.

[km², square kilometer]

Station number	Station name for upstream watershed	Upstream drainage area (km²)	Number of permitted outfalls	Number of outfalls for major facilities[1]
1	Fall Creek near Fortville	447	20	2
2	Eel River near Logansport	2,043	81	28
3	Tippecanoe River at Winimac	2,438	61	9
4	Wildcat Creek near Lafayette	2,056	96	33
5	Wabash River at Terre Haute	31,936	587	191
6	Mills Creek at Cagles Mill Dam	759	17	0
7	White River near Centerton	6,324	401	182
8	White River at Nora	3,149	235	105
9	Sugar Creek near New Palestine	243	9	1
10	East Fork Whitewater River near Brookville	986	31	9
11	Vernon Fork Muscatatuck River at Vernon	512	13	5
12	East Fork White River at Seymour	6,056	225	53
13	Blue River at Fredericksburg	732	18	2
14	Patoka River at Winslow	1,559	162	8
15	White River at Petersburg	28,794	1,009	140
16	Busseron Creek near Carlisle	591	155	9
17	Mississinewa River near Peoria	2,093	135	38
18	Wabash River near Huntington	1,985	49	14
19	Maumee River at New Haven	5,077	182	67
20	Fish Creek near Artic	248	2	0
21	St. Joseph River at Elkhart	8,756	170	51
22	Trail Creek at Michigan City	152	10	6
23	Deep River at Lake George at Hobart	321	21	7
24	Kankakee River at Shelby	4,597	94	45
25	Wabash River at Vincennes	35,628	100	34
26	Wabash River at Mt. Carmel, Ill.	74,293	261	5

[1] A major facility has the capacity to discharge more than 1 million gallons per day.

- Minelands: Bare sand/rock/clay, quarries/strip mines/ gravel pits, coal minelands, and transitional.

- Wetlands: Woody wetlands and emergent herbaceous wetlands.

- Open water.

- Grassland/herbaceous.

- Agricultural: Orchards/vineyards/other, pasture/hay, rowcrop, small grains, fallow.

For each of the 26 watersheds, the land area and the percentage of the drainage area in each land-cover type were determined (table 15). More than half of the drainage area in 24 of these 26 watersheds is in the agricultural land-cover type; the exceptions are watersheds 16 and 22.

Four of the land-cover types are of interest for their potential relation to mercury in watersheds: urban, forest, minelands, and wetlands. Urban land cover includes residential and commercial/industrial/transportation classes. All of the watersheds had area with urban land cover, although three watersheds had less than 1 percent. Forest land cover includes deciduous, evergreen, and mixed forest classes. The deciduous forest class was the most common; the shrubland land-cover class was uncommon. All of the watersheds had area with forest land cover. Minelands includes quarries, gravel pits, and active and abandoned (reclaimed and unreclaimed) surface coal mines. There are no gold or mercury mines in Indiana. Seven of the watersheds had more than 0.25 percent mineland, mostly coal mines, and one watershed had by far the most (19.6 percent). Wetlands land cover includes woody and emergent herbaceous wetlands. More than half the watersheds had greater than 1 percent of the area in wetlands, but the percentages generally were small—0.07 to 7.73 percent (table 15).

The percentages and areas of the 7 land-cover types were not correlated with average concentrations of total or methylmercury, percent methylmercury, average annual atmospheric mercury loading rates, stream mercury yields, or median dry-weight mercury concentrations in fish tissue samples in the 26 watersheds (Kendall's tau test). The differences among watersheds in these measures of mercury levels were demonstrated with graphical and statistical evaluations in earlier sections of this report. Therefore, in the absence of a statistical correlation, a weight-of-evidence approach was used to determine whether land-cover type corresponds with the apparent mercury levels in the watersheds.

The percentage of a watershed drainage area in a land-cover type does not take into account the square kilometers of area involved or the distribution and continuity of that land-cover type in a watershed, so two types of information were used to interpret and compare the percentages of land-cover types: drainage-area category and map image. The 26 watersheds were grouped into small, medium, and large categories on the basis of the size of the upstream drainage area: less

than 1,000 km²; from 1,000 to 10,000 km²; and more than 10,000 km² (table 16). The boundaries of the watersheds were mapped with color-coded land-cover types (fig. 17).

A high percentage of urban land corresponds with the high levels of mercury in watershed 7, the White River watershed in central Indiana. Watershed 7 is 12.6 percent urban (table 15), the highest percentage among medium-size watersheds (table 16, fig. 17). Watershed 8 is nested in watershed 7 and is 6.43 percent urban, the second-highest percentage among medium-size watersheds. Watershed 7 had total mercury concentrations that were among the highest (table 3). It also had a stream mercury yield that was higher than the atmospheric mercury wet- and dry-deposition loading (table 12). Consistent with the urban population and urban land use in watersheds 7 and 8, mercury was reported in nearly all of the 131 wastewater-effluent samples from 14 POTWs in these watersheds (table 13). Watershed 7 had 401 wastewater outfalls with 182 of them at major facilities (table 14).

A mapped density of urban land cover upstream from station 19 in the Maumee River watershed in northeastern Indiana (fig. 17) corresponds with the high mercury concentrations in water there (table 3) that were significantly higher than at other stations. Consistent with the urban population and urban land use upstream from station 19, a high average mercury concentration was reported for the 39 wastewater-effluent samples collected upstream (table 13). Watershed 19 had 182 wastewater outfalls and 67 of them were at major facilities (table 14).

Other studies support the potential influence of urban land cover on mercury in a watershed. High total mercury concentrations in Indiana streams, 2004–2006, were reported at stations with upstream watersheds that included urban and industrial wastewater discharges (Ulberg and Risch, 2008). Lyons and others (2006) reported that particulate mercury loads in the Scioto River in Ohio were higher in areas with urban activity compared to rural areas. Brightbill and others (2004) examined the correlations between total mercury and methylmercury in fish and water in the Delaware River Basin in New Jersey, New York, and Pennsylvania. They reported a positive correlation of total mercury concentrations in water and fish with urban land cover, population density, and percent impervious surfaces. Engstrom and others (2007) used age-dated sediment cores from 55 lakes in Minnesota to observe that modern mercury loading from atmospheric deposition was higher in urban areas than in rural areas.

A high percentage of forest land cover corresponds with the high mercury concentrations in water of the Patoka River watershed in southern Indiana (table 3); these concentrations were significantly higher than other stations. Watershed 14 is 39.3 percent forest (the highest percentage among all 26 watersheds; table 15). The estimated atmospheric mercury dry-deposition loading rate of 13.6 µg/m² was the highest (table 12), and the average annual mercury wet-deposition loading rate of 12.3 µg/m² was one of the highest (table 10). Watershed 14 does not have high annual mercury emissions or a high number of wastewater outfalls compared to other

Table 15. Land-cover types, by percentage of watershed drainage area and land area in watersheds upstream from monitoring stations on Indiana streams (from 2001 National Land Cover Database)

[pct, percentage of upstream drainage area, km², square kilometer]

Station number	Urban (pct)	Urban (km²)	Forest (pct)	Forest (km²)	Mineland (pct)	Mineland (km²)	Wetland (pct)	Wetland (km²)	Water (pct)	Water (km²)	Grassland (pct)	Grassland (km²)	Agricultural (pct)	Agricultural (km²)
1	5.23	23	5.45	24	0.11	<1	0.87	4	0.17	1	0	0	88.2	394
2	.92	19	8.28	169	0	0	1.63	33	.59	12	0	0	88.6	1,809
3	1.54	38	8.92	217	0	0	3.85	94	2.09	51	.01	0	83.6	2,039
4	3.29	68	3.10	64	.01	<1	1.19	24	.34	7	0	0	92.1	1,893
5	1.85	590	8.63	2,757	.32	102	1.70	543	.81	259	.39	124	86.3	27,459
6	.81	6	15.3	116	.23	2	.13	1	1.06	8	0	0	82.5	626
7	12.6	795	6.26	396	.11	7	.80	51	.94	60	0	0	79.3	5,015
8	6.43	203	4.07	128	.07	2	1.15	36	.72	23	0	0	87.5	2,757
9	1.95	5	4.97	12	0	0	.72	2	.23	1	0	0	92.1	224
10	3.55	35	17.4	171	0	0	.64	6	2.18	22	0	0	76.3	752
11	1.09	6	34.3	176	.34	2	.43	2	.44	2	0	0	63.4	325
12	2.90	176	8.74	530	.06	4	.76	46	.39	24	0	0	87.1	5,277
13	1.06	8	27.6	202	.06	<1	.07	1	.20	1	0	0	71.0	520
14	1.01	16	39.3	613	5.38	84	.75	12	2.70	42	0	0	50.9	709
15	4.22	1,215	23.9	6,884	1.27	366	.72	208	.95	273	0	0	68.9	19,482
16	2.11	12	25.4	150	19.6	116	6.35	37	2.20	13	4.63	27	39.7	119
17	2.91	61	7.36	154	.04	1	1.08	23	.84	18	0	0	87.8	1,837
18	1.31	26	5.60	111	.08	2	.75	15	2.92	58	0	0	89.3	1,773
19	4.17	212	9.97	506	.03	2	1.96	99	.74	38	.04	2	83.1	4,218
20	.62	2	18.1	45	.11	<1	3.66	9	2.04	5	.44	1	75.0	186
21	2.11	184	15.0	1,313	.03	3	6.01	527	2.82	247	.01	1	74.0	6,482
22	13.3	20	38.4	58	.08	<10	7.73	12	.89	1	6.21	9	33.3	51

Table 15. Land-cover types, by percentage of watershed drainage area and land area in watersheds upstream from monitoring stations on Indiana streams (from 2001 National Land Cover Database).—Continued

[pct, percentage of upstream drainage area; km², square kilometer]

Station number	Urban (pct)	Urban (km²)	Forest (pct)	Forest (km²)	Mineland (pct)	Mineland (km²)	Wetland (pct)	Wetland (km²)	Water (pct)	Water (km²)	Grassland (pct)	Grassland (km²)	Agricultural (pct)	Agricultural (km²)
23	18.7	60	18.1	58	0	0	3.76	12	1.34	4	4.16	13	54.0	173
24	1.93	89	11.2	515	.08	3	3.06	140	1.04	48	2.08	96	80.6	3,705
25	1.87	666	9.69	3,454	.79	281	1.97	701	.94	335	.48	173	84.2	29,736
26	2.70	2,005	16.1	11,973	1.24	921	1.57	1,168	.96	714	.28	211	77.1	56,380

watersheds (appendix table 1–5; table 14). Therefore, mercury in regional or continental air masses likely contributed to the high mercury wet- and dry-deposition loading to forest land cover in this watershed. Litterfall and throughfall are the potential pathways transporting mercury from the forest to the water.

Other studies support the potential influence of forest land cover on mercury in a watershed. Forests have been described as a sink for atmospheric mercury deposition and mercury accumulation (Lindberg, 1996; St. Louis and others, 2001; Grigal, 2002; Rea and others, 2002; Miller and others, 2005). Mercury deposition to forest land cover has been demonstrated to be higher than deposition to nonforest land cover, because the dry-deposition rate is higher in forests.

Other studies reported the potential influence of wetland abundance on total and methylmercury concentrations in water (St. Louis and others, 1994; Hurley and others, 1995; Brigham and others, 2009; Scudder and others, 2009). A significant correlation was not observed for Indiana watersheds, however, when the percentages of wetlands were compared with the average total and methylmercury concentrations and percentages of methylmercury. The absence of significant correlation may be due to the low percentage of wetland land cover in the Indiana watersheds (less than 7.7 percent; table 15), although it is unclear whether a significant correlation corresponds to a threshold of wetland abundance. The study areas in Brigham and others (2009) correlated mercury concentrations in water to wetland abundance of 13.2 to 35.6 percent. Brightbill and others (2004) and Krabbenhoft and others (1999) identified weak or nonsignificant correlations of mercury concentrations in water and wetland abundance.

Table 16.   Watersheds upstream from monitoring stations on Indiana streams, grouped by upstream drainage-area size.

[km², square kilometer; <, less than; >, greater than]

Drainage-area size category	Station number	Station name	Upstream drainage area (km²)
Small (< 1,000 km²)	22	Trail Creek at Michigan City	152
	9	Sugar Creek near New Palestine	243
	20	Fish Creek near Artic	248
	23	Deep River at Lake George-Hobart	321
	1	Fall Creek near Fortville	447
	11	Vernon Fk Muscatatuck R at Vernon	512
	16	Busseron Creek near Carlisle	591
	13	Blue River at Fredericksburg	732
	6	Mills Creek at Cagles Mill Dam	759
	10	East Fork Whitewater R near Brookville	986
Medium (1,000 km² to 10,000 km²)	14	Patoka River at Winslow	1,559
	18	Wabash River near Huntington	1,985
	2	Eel River near Adamsboro	2,043
	4	Wildcat Creek near Lafayette	2,056
	17	Mississinewa River near Peoria	2,093
	3	Tippecanoe River at Winimac	2,438
	8	White River at Nora	3,149
	24	Kankakee River at Shelby	4,597
	19	Maumee River at New Haven	5,077
	12	East Fork White River at Seymour	6,056
	7	White River at Centerton	6,324
	21	St. Joseph River at Elkhart	8,756
Large (> 10,000 km²)	15	White River at Petersburg	28,794
	5	Wabash River at Terre Haute	31,936
	25	Wabash River at Vincennes	35,628
	26	Wabash River at Mt. Carmel, Ill.	74,293

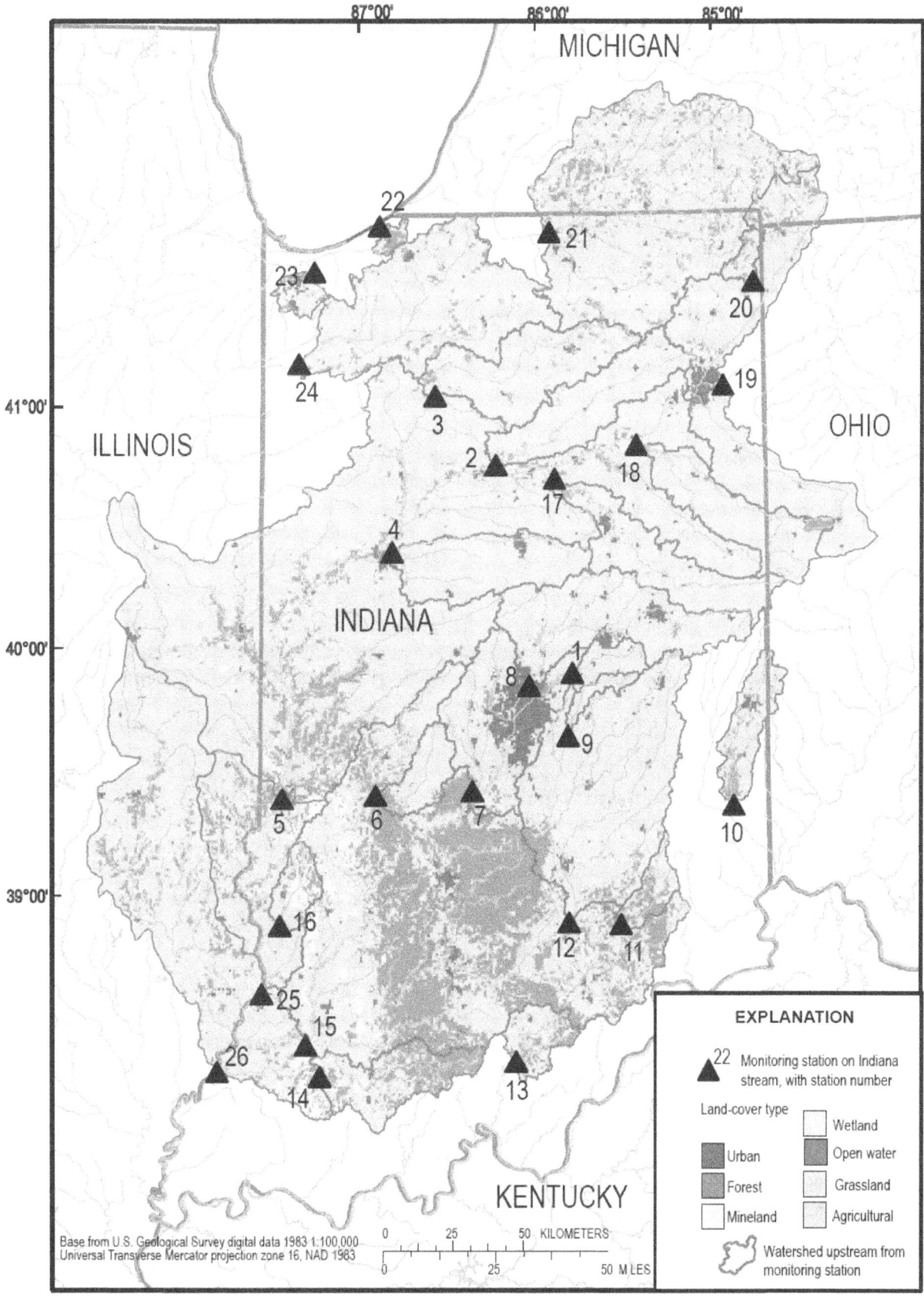

Figure 17.   Land-cover types in watersheds upstream from monitoring stations on Indiana streams (from 2001 National Land Cover Database).

Summary and Conclusions

This report presents a retrospective view of mercury in Indiana watersheds for 2001–2006 and interprets the ways sources of mercury influence mercury concentrations in water, stream mercury yields, and mercury concentrations in fish. More than 384,000 data values were assembled and computed from mercury-monitoring records, mercury-source inventories, ancillary data (instantaneous streamflow, daily average streamflow, and daily precipitation), and maps of land-cover classes. A natural hydrologic boundary was used to group the data that were analyzed, defined by the drainage area (watershed) upstream from each of 26 monitoring stations for mercury in streams. These watersheds range from 152 km² to 74,293 km² in area and drain approximately 79.5 percent of the land area of Indiana.

Unfiltered total mercury concentrations reported in 411 water samples, 2002–2006, had a median of 2.32 ng/L and a maximum of 28.2 ng/L. The percentage of total mercury concentrations that equaled or exceeded Indiana water-quality criteria were 5.4 percent for the 12-ng/L chronic-aquatic criterion, 59 percent for the 1.8-ng/L Great Lakes human-health criterion, and 72.5 percent for the 1.3-ng/L Great Lakes wildlife criterion.

Three monitoring stations had the most samples with total mercury concentrations higher than water-quality criteria, the highest maximum concentrations, and the most concentrations higher than the 90th percentile: station 7, White River near Centerton in central Indiana; station 14, Patoka River at Winslow in southern Indiana; and station 19, Maumee River at New Haven in northeast Indiana. Total mercury concentrations at these stations were significantly higher than those at other stations. Interpretations of the geographic differences in mercury concentrations were not confounded by any seasonal patterns or long-term trends. Overall, unfiltered and filtered total mercury concentrations tended to be highest when instantaneous streamflow at the time of sample collection was highest.

On average, 67 percent of the total mercury in all samples was particulate (determined by subtracting filtered from unfiltered concentrations). Particulate total mercury concentrations showed a strong positive correlation with turbidity in water samples, and nearly all that exceeded the 12-ng/L chronic-aquatic criterion were associated with turbidity higher than 60 NTRU. Turbidity tended to be highest when instantaneous streamflow was highest. Particulate total mercury was significantly lower in samples collected downstream from dams.

Unfiltered methylmercury as a percentage of unfiltered total mercury ranged from 0.4 to 64.8 percent, with a median of 3.7 percent. Percentages of methylmercury in samples at five monitoring stations downstream from dams were significantly higher than at 20 other stations.

Annual stream mercury yields, 2002–2006, were computed with a model by using the mercury concentrations in the streams and the daily average streamflows, normalized to the watershed area. Estimates of 89 annual stream yields of total mercury at 18 stations ranged from 0.47 to 78.9 µg/m²/yr, with a median of 3.47 µg/m²/yr. The 5-year average annual stream yield of total mercury ranged from 0.73 to 45.2 µg/m²/yr, with a median of 4.22 µg/m²/yr. The median annual stream yield of methylmercury was 1.9 percent of the median annual stream yield of total mercury. The highest average annual stream yields of total mercury were 39.6 µg/m²/yr from watershed 7, White River near Centerton; and 45.2 µg/m²/yr from watershed 12, East Fork White River near Seymour.

Mercury concentrations in fish tissue were evaluated for 1,731 samples from 59 lakes and reservoirs and 358 rivers and streams in the 26 watersheds (83 percent of the sites statewide for 1993–2004). Wet-weight concentrations had a median of 130 µg/kg, and 12.4 percent of samples exceeded the 300-µg/kg USEPA methylmercury criterion. A coarse-scale review of all fish-tissue samples and a fine-scale review of samples within 5 km of the downstream end of watersheds indicated that fish mercury concentrations were highest in watershed 15, White River at Petersburg and watershed 1, Fall Creek near Fortville. Near the downstream end of watershed 15, 45 percent of wet-weight mercury concentrations were greater than the USEPA methylmercury criterion; the next highest proportion greater than the criterion was 40 percent in watershed 1.

A GIS grid map of atmospheric mercury wet-deposition rates for 2001–2006 was made with average annual precipitation data from 151 National Weather Service Cooperative Observer Program sites and average annual mercury concentration data from 9 National Atmospheric Deposition Program Mercury Deposition Network (MDN) stations in and around Indiana. The average annual atmospheric mercury wet-deposition loading rates were computed for each watershed and ranged from 9.60 to 14.8 µg/m²/yr, with a median of 11.3 µg/m²/yr. Four watersheds in southern Indiana had wet-deposition loading rates higher than the statewide average of 12 µg/m²/yr.

Atmospheric mercury dry-deposition rates were estimated with an inferential method by using concentrations of three mercury species measured in air samples at three MDN sites in Indiana in 2004. Seasonal mercury dry-deposition rates were summed for forest and nonforest land cover in each watershed to obtain annual loadings. Estimated annual atmospheric mercury dry-deposition loading rates to the watersheds ranged from 5.6 µg/m²/yr (watershed 4) to 13.6 µg/m²/yr (watershed 14). The median was 7.2 µg/m²/yr. Dry-deposition loading rates were 0.49 to 1.4 times the wet-deposition loading rates.

The average annual stream mercury yields were less than 100 percent of combined atmospheric mercury wet and dry-deposition loadings in 14 watersheds. The stream yield to atmospheric loading ratio was 224 percent for watershed 7, White River near Centerton, and 233 percent for watershed 12, East Fork White River near Seymour, indicating that sources other than atmospheric deposition contributed to the stream mercury yield. Some of the mercury in these two watersheds potentially was contributed by wastewater discharges.

Total mercury was detected in 96 percent of 402 waste-water-effluent samples from publicly owned treatment works in the 26 watersheds, 2002–2005, and ranged from <0.05 to 88 ng/L, with a median of 2.9 ng/L. The 12-ng/L Indiana chronic-aquatic criterion was equaled or exceeded by 12 percent of the concentrations; 68 percent equaled or exceeded the 1.8-ng/L Great Lakes human-health criterion, and 81 percent equaled or exceeded the 1.3-ng/L Great Lakes wildlife criterion. Mercury was reported in nearly all of the samples of wastewater effluent from watersheds 7, 12, and 19.

There were 4,144 permitted outfalls of treated and untreated wastewater effluent in the 26 watersheds in 2005, including 1,044 classified as outfalls of a major facility with the capacity to discharge up to 1 million gallons per day. Watershed 7 had 401 outfalls (45 percent at a major facility), watershed 12 had 225 outfalls (24 percent at major facility), and watershed 19 had 182 outfalls (37 percent at a major facility).

Land-cover type corresponded with measures of the apparent mercury levels in three watersheds. (1) Watershed 7, White River in central Indiana, had a high percentage of urban land cover and some of the highest total mercury concentrations and stream mercury yields. The urban land cover and numerous permitted wastewater outfalls (most with mercury detected in treated effluent) potentially contributed mercury to this watershed. (2) A monitoring station on the Maumee River in northeast Indiana, downstream from a large area of urban land cover, recorded the highest stream mercury concentrations. The urban land cover and mercury detected in treated effluent potentially contributed mercury to this watershed. (3) A watershed of the Patoka River in southern Indiana with a high percentage of forest land cover had the highest atmospheric mercury dry-deposition rate. The forest land cover contributed to the high dry-deposition rate that potentially contributed mercury to this watershed.

In conclusion, this study showed that total mercury in Indiana watersheds can be attributed mostly to wet and dry deposition of atmospheric mercury. Total mercury in some watersheds also can be attributed to discharges of mercury in wastewater. Total mercury concentrations in streams are moderately correlated to the number of mercury-emission sources in the watershed and their annual emissions of mercury, as well as to the number of wastewater outfalls in the watershed.

Regulatory programs for air quality and water quality in Indiana will need long-term monitoring data for detecting changes in mercury concentrations and stream yields resulting from reductions in mercury emissions and mercury discharges. Future monitoring that includes mercury in precipitation, air samples, litterfall, and throughfall; mercury in streams and reservoirs; and mercury in fish tissue would yield data for comparison with the 2001–2006 data presented in this report. Future inventories of mercury-emission sources, annual emissions, wastewater outfalls, and mercury concentrations in wastewater could be compared with the 2001–2006 baseline in this report.

Interpretations presented in this report provide a perspective for identifying modifications in future monitoring that likely would reduce limitations and uncertainties in future interpretations, including the following.

- Investigation of mercury in water from reservoirs in Indiana would help to explain the locations, conditions, and timing that affect percentages of methylmercury in water downstream.

- Coordination of mercury monitoring in fish tissue with mercury monitoring in water would improve the capability for correlating mercury concentrations in fish with mercury concentrations in water and with stream mercury loads in Indiana watersheds.

- Adjustment of the stream-monitoring stations in the statewide network to locations where streamflow is not impeded by dams or by flow stagnation/flow reversals would allow stream mercury loads to be computed for all stations in the network.

- Adjustment of the locations of stream-monitoring stations in the statewide network to sites with a more uniform range of upstream drainage areas may result in refined assessments of correlations between mercury sources and mercury concentrations in water and fish.

- Direct analysis of particulate total and methylmercury would reduce the uncertainty in concentrations (which were determined for this report by subtracting filtered from unfiltered concentrations).

- Analysis of methylmercury with a consistent reporting limit of 0.05 ng/L would reduce the uncertainty associated with censored values that have inconsistent reporting limits.

- Analysis of supplementary constituents in water analyzed for mercury—specifically, suspended sediment, dissolved organic carbon, and sulfate—would improve the capability for interpreting the sources and transport of mercury and methylmercury in watersheds.

- Investigation of the flow volumes and mercury concentrations in wastewater effluent, during conditions ranging from base flow to stormflow, would help to characterize the relative importance of mercury in wastewater discharges compared to atmospheric mercury deposition loading.

- Establishment of a monitoring station for mercury in precipitation in southwestern Indiana would increase the resolution for mapping atmospheric wet-deposition rates. This information could clarify the effect of atmospheric mercury loading on stream mercury loads and mercury in fish in this part of the State.

- Establishment of long-term monitoring for dry deposition of atmospheric mercury—including analysis of mercury concentrations in air, litterfall, throughfall and surrogate surfaces—would improve the calculation and modeling of atmospheric mercury dry-deposition loading to watersheds.

References

Alpers, C.N., Stewart, A.R., Saiki, M.K., Marvin-DiPasquale, M.C., Topping, B.R., Rider, K.M., Gallanthine, S.K., Kester, C.A., Rye, R.O., Antweiler, R.C., and De Wild, J.F., 2008, Environmental factors affecting mercury in Camp Far West Reservoir, California, 2001–03: U.S. Geological Survey Scientific Investigations Report 2006–5008, 358 p.

American Meteorological Society, 2000, Glossary of meteorology (2d ed.), accessed August 2007 at *http://amsglossary. allenpress.com/glossary.*

American Public Health Association, American Water Works Association, and Water Environment Federation, 1992, Standard methods for the examination of water and wastewater (18th ed.): Washington, D.C., American Public Health Association, p. 2–60 to 2–63.

Babiarz, C.L., Hurley, J.P., Benoit, J.M., Shafer, M.M., Andren, A.W., and Webb, D.A., 1998, Seasonal influences on partitioning and transport of total and methylmercury in rivers from contrasting watersheds: Biogeochemistry, v. 41, no. 3, p. 237–257.

Balogh, S.J., and Liang, L., 1995, Mercury pathways in municipal wastewater treatment plants: Water, Air, and Soil Pollution, v. 80, p. 1181–1190.

Balogh, S.J., Meyer, M.L., and Johnson, K.K., 1997, Mercury and suspended sediment loadings in the Lower Minnesota River: Environmental Science & Technology, v. 31, no. 1, p. 198–202.

Bell, A.H., and Scudder, B.C., 2007, Mercury accumulation in periphyton of eight river ecosystems: Journal of the American Water Resources Association, v. 43, no. 4, p. 957–968.

Bodaly, R.A.; Beaty, K.G.; Hendzel, L.H.; Majewski, A.R.; Paterson, M.J.; Rolfhus, K.R.; Penn, A.F.; St. Louis, V.L.; Hall, B.D.; Matthews, C.J.D.; Cherewyk, K.A.; Mailman, Mariah; Hurley, J.P.; Schiff, S.L.; and Venkiteswaran, J.J., 2004, Experimenting with hydroelectric reservoirs: Environmental Science & Technology, v. 38, no. 18, p. 346A–352A.

Bodaly, R.A., Jansen, W.A., Majewski, A.R., Fudge, R.J.P., Strange, N.E., Derksen, A.J., and Green, D.J., 2007, Postimpoundment time course of increased mercury concentrations in fish in hydroelectric reservoirs of northern Manitoba, Canada: Archive of Environmental Contamination and Toxicology, v. 53, no. 3, p. 379–389.

Brigham, M.E., Wentz, D.A., Aiken, G.R., and Krabbenhoft, D.P., 2009, Mercury cycling in stream ecosystems. 1. Water column chemistry and transport: Environmental Science & Technology, v. 43, no. 8, p. 2720–2725.

Brightbill, R.A.; Riva-Murray, Karen; Bilger, M.D.; and Byrnes, J.D., 2004, Total mercury and methylmercury in fish fillets, water, and bed sediments from selected streams in the Delaware River Basin, New Jersey, New York, and Pennsylvania, 1998–2001: U.S. Geological Survey Water-Resources Investigations Report 03–4183, 30 p.

Chasar, L.C., Scudder, B.B., Stewart, A.R., Bell, A.H., and Aiken, G.R., 2009, Mercury cycling in stream ecosystems. 3. Tophic dynamics and methylmercury accumulation: Environmental Science & Technology, v. 43, no. 8, p. 2733–2739.

Clark, G.D., ed., 1980, The Indiana water resource—Availability, uses, and needs: Indianapolis, Indiana Department of Natural Resources, 1,508 p.

Cocca, Paul, 2001, Mercury maps—A quantitative spatial link between air deposition and fish tissue: U.S. Environmental Protection Agency Office of Water, EPA–823–R–01–009, 31 p.

Cohen, Mark; Artz, Richard; Draxler, Roland; Miller, Paul; Poissant, Laurier; Niemi, David; Ratté, Dominique; Deslauriers, Marc; Duval, Roch; Laurin, Rachelle; Slotnick, Jennifer; Nettesheim, Todd; and McDonald, John, 2004, Modeling the atmospheric transport and deposition of mercury to the Great Lakes: Environmental Research, v. 95, no. 3, p. 247–265.

Eaton, N.K., 2002, Abandoned mine lands, miscellaneous site features in Indiana, 1:24,000, polygon shapefile vector digital data. Bloomington, Ind., Indiana Geological Survey, accessed August 2007 at *http://igs.indiana.edu/arcims/ statewide/download.html.*

Engstrom, D.R., Balogh, S.J., and Swain, E.B., 2007, History of inputs to Minnesota lakes—Influences of watershed disturbance and localized atmospheric deposition: Limnology and Oceanography, v. 52, no. 6, p. 2467–2483.

Environmental Systems Research Institute, Inc., 2006, ArcGIS version 9.2.

Evers, D.C., 2005, Mercury connections—The extent and effects of mercury pollution in northeastern North America: Gorham, Maine, Biodiversity Research Institute, 29 p.

Fan, P.L., Batchu, H., Chou, H.-N., Gasparac, W., Sandrik, J., and Meyer, D.M., 2002, Laboratory evaluation of amalgam separators: Journal of the American Dental Association, v. 133, no. 5, p. 577–584.

Fitzgerald, W.F., Engstrom, D.R., Mason, R.P., and Nater, E.A., 1998, The case for atmospheric mercury contamination in remote areas: Environmental Science & Technology, v. 32. no. 1, p. 1–7.

Frans, L.M., and Helsel, D.R., 2005, Evaluating regional trends in ground-water nitrate concentrations of the Colombia Basin Ground Water Management Area, Washington: U.S. Geological Survey Scientific Investigations Report 2005–5078, 7 p.

Grigal, D.F., 2002, Inputs and outputs of mercury from terrestrial wasteds—A review: National Research Council of Canada Environmental Reviews, v. 10, no. 1, p. 1–39.

Hall, B.D., St. Louis, V.L., Rolfhus, K.R., Bodaly, R.A., Beaty, K.G., Paterson, M.J., and Peech Cherewyk, K.A., 2005, Impacts of reservoir creation on the biogeochemical cycling of methyl mercury and total mercury in boreal upland forests: Ecosystems, v. 8, no 3, p. 248–266.

Harris, R.C., Krabbenhoft, D.P., Mason, R.P., Murray, M.W., Reash, R., and Saltman, T., eds., 2007, Ecosystem responses to mercury contamination—Indicators of change: Pensacola, Fla., Society of Environmental Toxicology and Chemistry Press, 216 p.

Harris, R.C.; Rudd, J.W.M.; Amyot, Marc; Babiarz, C.L.; Beaty K.G.; Blanchfield P.J.; Bodaly, R.A.; Branfireun, B.A.; Gilmour, C.C.; Graydon, J.A.; Heyes, Andrew; Hintelmann, Holger; Hurley, J.P.; Kelly, C.A.; Krabbenhoft, D.P.; Lindberg, S.E.; Mason, R.P.; Paterson, M.J.; Podemski, C.L.; Robinson, Art; Sandilands, K.A.; Southworth, G.R.; St. Louis, V.L.; and Tate M.T., 2007, Whole-ecosystem study shows rapid fish-mercury response to changes in mercury deposition: Proceedings of the National Academy of Sciences, v. 104, no. 42, p. 16586–16591.

Helsel, D.R., 2005, Nondetects and data analysis—Statistics for censored environmental data: Hoboken, N.J., Wiley-Interscience, 250 p.

Helsel, D.R., and Hirsch, R.M., 1995, Statistical methods in water resources (2d printing): Amsterdam, Elsevier Science Publishers, 529 p.

Helsel, D.R., Mueller, D.K., and Slack, J.R., 2006, Computer program for the Kendall family of trend tests: U.S. Geological Survey Scientific Investigations Report 2005–5275, 4 p.

Hintelmann, Holger; Harris, Reed; Heyes, Andrew; Hurley, J.P.; Kelly, C.A.; Krabbenhoft, D.P.; Lindberg, Steve; Rudd, J.W.M.; Scott, K.J.; and St. Louis, V.L., 2002, Reactivity and mobility of new and old mercury deposition in a boreal forest ecosystem during the first year of the METAALICUS study: Environmental Science & Technology, v. 36, no. 23, p. 5034–5040.

Hirsch, R.M., Slack, J.R., and Smith, R.A., 1982, Techniques of trend analysis for monthly water quality data: Water Resources Research, v. 18, no. 1, p. 107–121.

Horowitz, A.J., 1991, A primer on sediment-trace element chemistry (2d ed.): Chelsea, Mich., Lewis Publishers, 136 p.

Hurley, J.P., Benoit, J.M., Babiarz, C.L., Shafer, M.M., Andren, A.W., Sullivan, J.R., Hammond, Richard, and Webb, D.A., 1995, Influences of watershed characteristics on mercury levels in Wisconsin rivers: Environmental Science & Technology, v. 29, no, 7, p. 1867–1875.

Hurley, J.P., Cowell, S.E., Shafer, M.M., and Hughes, P.E., 1998, Tributary loading of mercury to Lake Michigan—Importance of seasonal events and phase partitioning: Science of the Total Environment, v. 213, no. 1–3, p. 129–137.

Indiana Administrative Code, 2007a, Title 327, Article 2, Rule 1, Minimum Surface Water Quality Standards, Section 6 (a)(3), table 6–1, Surface water quality criteria for specific substances: Accessed August 2007 at *http://www.in.gov/ legislative/iac/T03270/A00020.PDF*.

Indiana Administrative Code, 2007b, Title 327, Article 2, Rule 1.5, Water Quality Standards Applicable to All State Waters Within the Great Lakes System, Section 8, Minimum Surface Water Quality Criteria, table 8–3, Water-quality criteria for protection of human health, and table 8–4, Water-quality criteria for protection of wildlife: Accessed August 2007 at*http://www.in.gov/legislative/iac/T03270/A00020.PDF*.

Indiana Business Research Center, 2009, STATS Indiana: Indiana University Kelley School of Business, accessed February 2009 at *http://www.stats.indiana.edu.*

Indiana Department of Environmental Management, 2006, Indiana integrated water quality monitoring and assessment report: accessed August 2007 at *http://www.in.gov/idem/ programs/water/305b/2006integrept/ir_narrative.doc.*

Indiana Geological Survey, 2002, Surface coal mines in Indiana: Bloomington, Ind., Indiana Geological Survey, 1:24,000 polygon shapefile, accessed August 2007 at *http:// igs.indiana.edu/arcims/statewide/download.html.*

Indiana State Department of Health, 2007, Indiana fish consumption advisory, accessed December 2007 at *http://www. state.in.us/isdh/dataandstats/fish/2007/index.htm.*

Indiana State Department of Health, Indiana Department of Environmental Management, and Indiana Department of Natural Resources, 2006, Indiana fish consumption advisory: 24 p.

Indiana Department of Natural Resources, 2007, Indiana statewide outdoor recreation plan 2006–2010, accessed February 2009 at *http://www.in.gov/dnr/outdoor/4201.htm.*

Insightful Corporation, 2005, S-PLUS 7.0 for Windows, Professional Developer.

Keeler, G.J., Landis, M.S., Norris, G.A., Christianson, E.M., and Dvonch, J.T., 2006, Sources of mercury wet deposition in eastern Ohio, USA: Environmental Science & Technology, v. 40, no. 19, p. 5874–5881.

Kelly, C.A. Rudd, J.W.M., Bodaly, R.A., Roulet, N.P., St. Louis, V.L., Heyes, A., Moore, T.R., Schiff, S., Aravena, R., Scott, K.J., Dyck, B., Harris, R., Warner, B., and Edwards, G.,1997, Increases in fluxes of greenhouse gases and methyl mercury following flooding of an experimental reservoir: Environmental Science & Technology, v. 31, no. 5, p. 1334–1344.

Kendall, M.G., 1970, Rank correlation methods (4th ed.): London, Charles Griffin, 202 p.

Krabbenhoft, D.P., and Rickert, D.A., 1995, Mercury contamination of aquatic ecosystems: U.S. Geological Survey Fact Sheet FS–216–95, 4 p.

Krabbenhoft, D.P., Wiener, J.G., Brumbaugh, W.G., Olson, M.L., DeWild, J.F., and Sabin, T.J., 1999, A national pilot study of mercury contamination of aquatic ecosystems along multiple gradients, *in* Morganwalp, D.W., and Buxton, H.T., eds., U.S. Geological Survey Toxic Substances Hydrology Program—Proceedings of the Technical Meeting, Charleston, S.C., March 8–12, 1999, v. 2 *of* 3, Contamination of hydrologic systems and related ecosystems: U.S. Geological Survey Water-Resources Investigations Report 99–4018B, p. 147–160.

Lindberg, S.E., 1996, Forests and the global biogeochemical cycle of mercury—The importance of understanding air/ vegetation exchange processes, *in* Baeyens, W., Ebinghaus, R., and Vasiliev, O., eds., Global and regional mercury cycles—Sources, fluxes and mass balances: Dordrecht, Netherlands, Kluwer Academic Publishers, NATO ASI Series, v. 21, p. 359–380.

Lyman, S.N., Gustin, M.A., Prestbo, E.M., and Marsik, F.J., 2007, Estimation of dry deposition of atmospheric mercury in Nevada by direct and indirect methods: Environmental Science & Technology, v. 41, no. 6, p. 1970–1976.

Lyons, W.B., Fitzgibbon, T.O., Welch, K.A., and Carey, A.E., 2006, Mercury geochemistry of the Scioto River, Ohio— Impact of agriculture and urbanization: Applied Geochemistry, v. 21, no. 11, p. 1880–1888.

Mann, H.B., 1945, Non-parametric tests against trend: Econometrica, v. 13, no. 3, p. 245–259.

Marvin-DiPasquale, Mark; Lutz, M.A.; Brigham, M.E.; Krabbenhoft, D.P.; Aiken, G.R.; Orem, W.H.; and Hall, B.D., 2009, Mercury cycling stream ecosystems. 2. Benthic methylmercury production and bed sediment–pore water partitioning: Environmental Science & Technology, v. 43, no. 8, p. 2726–2732.

Mason, R.P.; Abbott, M.L.; Bodaly, R.A.; Bullock, O.R., Jr.; Driscoll, C.T.; Evers, David; Lindberg, S.E.; Murray, Michael; and Swain, E.B., 2005, Monitoring the response to changing mercury deposition: Environmental Science & Technology, v. 39, no. 1, p. 14A–22A

Mason, R.P., and Sullivan, K.A., 1998, Mercury and methylmercury transport through an urban watershed: Water Research, v. 32, no. 2, p. 321–330.

Mergler, D., Anderson, H.A., Chan, L.H.M, Mahaffey, K.R., Murray, M., Sakamoto, M., and Stern., A.H., 2007, Methylmercury exposure and health effects in humans—A worlwide concern: Ambio, v. 26, no. 1, p. 3–11.

Midwestern Regional Climate Center, 2007, Online data, accessed December 2007 at *http://mcc.sws.uiuc.edu/.*

Miller, E.K.; Vanarsdale, Alan; Keeler, G.J.; Chalmers, Ann; Poissant, Laurier; Kamman, N.C.; and Brulotte, Raynald, 2005, Estimation and mapping of wet and dry mercury deposition across northeastern North America: Ecotoxicology, v. 14, no. 1–2, p. 53–70.

Morel, F.M.M., Kraepiel, A.M.L., and Amyot, Marc, 1998, The chemical cycle and bioaccumulation of mercury: Annual Review of Ecology and Systematics, v. 29, p. 543–566.

Morlock, S.E., Nguyen, H.T., and Majors, D.K., 2004, Water resources data, Indiana, water year 2003: U.S. Geological Survey Water-Data Report IN–03–1, 610 p.

Multi-Resolution Land Characteristics Consortium, 2001, National Land Cover Database 2001, data archive and description, accessed August 2007 at *http://www.mrlc.gov.*

Munthe, John; Bodaly, R.A.; Branfireun, B.A.; Driscoll, C.T.; Gilmour, C.C.; Harris, Reed; Horvat, Milena; Lucotte, Marc; and Malm, Olaf, 2007, Recovery of mercury-contaminated fisheries: Ambio, v. 36, no. 1, p. 33–44.

National Association of Clean Water Agencies, 2000, Evaluation of domestic sources of mercury by the Association of Metropolitan Sewerage Agencies, accessed February 2009 at *http://dev.nacwa.org/index.php?option=com_content& view=article&id=3563Aevaluation-of-domestic-sources-of-mercury-august-2000&catid=103Awatershed-water-quality&Itemid=17.*

National Atmospheric Deposition Program, 2007a, Mercury Deposition Network online data archive, accessed August 2007 at *http://nadp.sws.uiuc.edu/mdn.*

National Atmospheric Deposition Program, 2007b, Mercury Deposition Network concentration and deposition maps for 2003, 2004, 2005, and 2006, accessed August 2007 at *http://nadp.sws.uiuc.edu/mdn/maps.*

National Research Council, 2000, Toxicological effects of methylmercury: Washington, D.C., National Academy Press, Committee on the Toxicological Effects of Methylmercury, Board of Environmental Studies and Toxicology, 344 p.

Plourde, Yanick; Lucotte, Marc; and Pichet, Pierre, 1997, Contribution of suspended particulate matter and zooplankton to MeHg contamination of the food chain in midnorthern Quebec (Canada) reservoirs: Canadian Journal of Fisheries Aquatic Science, v. 54, no. 4, p. 821–831.

Poissant, Laurier; Pilote, Martin; Xu, Xiaohong; Zhang, Hong; and Beauvais, Conrad, 2004, Atmospheric mercury speciation and deposition in the Bay St. François wetlands: Journal of Geophysical Research D, Atmospheres, v. 109, no. 11, D11301, 11 p.

Purdue Applied Meteorology Group, 2005, Indiana climate page: Department of Agronomy, Plant, and Soils Lab, accessed August 2007 at *http://agmetx.agry.purdue.edu/sc.norm-geog.html.*

Rea, A.W., Lindberg, S.E., Scherbatskoy, T., and Keeler, G.J., 2002, Mercury accumulation in foliage over time in two northern mixed hardwood forests: Water, Air, and Soil Pollution, v. 133, p. 49–67.

Risch, M.R., 2005, Mercury in the Grand Calumet River/Indiana Harbor Canal and Lake Michigan, Lake County, Indiana, August 2001 and May 2002: U.S. Geological Survey Scientific Investigations Report 2005–5034, 46 p.

Risch, M.R., 2007, Mercury in precipitation in Indiana, January 2001–December 2003: U.S. Geological Survey Scientific Investigations Report 2007–5063, 76 p.

Risch, M.R., 2009, Monitoring program for mercury in precipitation in Indiana: Data summary for 2001–2007, accessed February 2009 at *http://in.water.usgs.gov/mercury/htdocs/ Mercury_ Precipitation_Summary_2001-2007.pdf.*

Risch, M.R., and Fowler, K.K, 2008, Mercury in precipitation in Indiana, January 2004–December 2005: U.S. Geological Survey Scientific Investigations Report 2008–5148, 76 p.

Risch, M.R., Prestbo, E.M., and Hawkins, Lucas, 2007, Measurement of atmospheric mercury species with manual sampling and analysis methods in a case study in Indiana: Water, Air, and Soil Pollution, v. 184, p. 285–297.

Runkel, R.L., Crawford, C.G., and Cohn, T.A., 2004, Load Estimator (LOADEST)—A FORTRAN program for estimating constituent loads in streams and rivers: U.S. Geological Survey Techniques and Methods, book 4, chap. A5, 69 p.

Schertz, T.L., Alexander, R.B., and Ohe, D.J., 1991, The computer program Estimate Trend (ESTREND), a system for the detection of trends in water-quality data: U.S. Geological Survey Water-Resources Investigations Report 91–4040, 63 p.

Scheuhammer, A.M., Meyer, M.W., Sandheinrich, M.B., and Murray, M.W., 2007, Effects of environmental methylmercury on the health of wild birds, mammals, and fish: Ambio, v. 36, no. 1, p. 12–18.

Schuster, P.F., Shanley, J.B., Marvin-DePasquale, M., Reddy, M.M., Aiken, G.R., Roth, D.A., Taylor, H.E., Krabbenhoft, D.P., and Dewild, J.F., 2007, Mercury and organic carbon dynamics during runoff episodes from a northeastern USA watershed: Water, Air, and Soil Pollution, v. 187, p. 89–108.

Scudder, B.C., Chasar, L.C., Wentz, D.A., Bauch, N.J., Brigham, M.E., Moran, P.W., and Krabbenhoft, D.P., 2009, Mercury in fish, bed sediment, and water from streams across the United States, 1998–2005: U.S. Geological Survey Scientific Investigations Report 2009–5109, 74 p.

Seigneur, Christian; Lohman, Kristen; Vijayaraghavan, Krish; Jansen, J.; and Levin, L., 2006, Modeling atmospheric deposition in the vicinity of power plants: Journal of Air and Waste Management Association, v. 56, no. 6, p. 743–751.

Seigneur, Christian; Vijayaraghavan, Krish; Lohman, Kristen; Karamchandani, Prakish; and Scott, Courtney, 2004, Global source attribution for mercury deposition in the United States: Environmental Science & Technology, v. 38, no. 2, p. 555–569.

Shanley, J.B.; Mast, M.A.; Campbell, D.H.; Aiken, G.R.; Krabbenhoft, D.P.; Hunt, R.J.; Walker, J.F.; Schuster, P.F.; Chalmers, Ann; Aulenbach, B.T.; Peters, N.E.; Marvin-DiPasquale, Mark; Clow, D.W.; and Shafer, M.M., 2008, Comparison of total mercury and methylmercury cycling at five sites using the small watershed approach: Environmental Pollution, v. 154, no. 1, p. 143–154.

St. Louis, V.L.; Rudd, J.W.M.; Kelly, C.A.; Beaty, K.G.; Bloom, N.S.; and Flett, R.J., 1994, Importance of wetlands as sources of methyl mercury to boreal forest ecosystems: Canadian Journal of Fisheries and Aquatic Sciences, v. 51, p. 1065–1076.

St. Louis, V.L.; Rudd, J.W.M.; Kelly, C.A.; Bodaly, R.A.; Paterson, M.J.; Beaty, K.G.; Hesslein, R.H.; Heyes, Andrew; and Majewski, A.R., 2004, The rise and fall of mercury methylation in an experimental reservoir: Environmental Science & Technology, v. 38, no. 5, p. 1348–1358.

St. Louis, V.L.; Rudd, J.W.M.; Kelly, C.A.; Hall, B.D.; Rolfhus, K.R.; Scott, K.J.; Lindberg, S.E.; and Dong, Weijin, 2001, Importance of the forest canopy to fluxes of methyl mercury and total mercury to boreal ecosystems: Environmental Science & Technology, v. 35, no. 15, p. 3089–3098.

Stahl, J.R., 1997, A preliminary appraisal of the biological integrity of Indiana streams in the West Fork White River Watershed using fish tissue contamination assessment: Indiana Department of Environmental Management, Office of Water Management, Assessment Branch, Biological Studies Section, IDEM/32/03/005/1997, 86 p.

Tibco Software, Inc., 2008, Spotfire S+ Version 8.1.

Ulberg, A.L., and Risch, M.R., 2008, Total mercury and methylmercury in Indiana streams, August 2004–September 2006: U.S. Geological Survey Scientific Investigations Report 2008–5176, 76 p.

U.S. Environmental Protection Agency, 1997, Mercury study report to Congress—Volume I. Exective summary: Office of Air Quality Planning and Standards and Office of Research and Development, EPA452/R–97–003, 95 p.

U.S. Environmental Protection Agency, 1999, The national survey of mercury concentrations in fish—Data base summary, 1990–1995: Office of Water Report EPA–823–R–99–014 [variously paginated].

U.S. Environmental Protection Agency, 2001, Water quality criterion for the protection of human health—Methylmercury: Office of Water Report EPA–823-R–01–001, accessed March 2009 at *http://www.epa.gov/waterscience/criteria/methylmercury*.

U.S. Environmental Protection Agency, 2008, Model-based analysis and tracking of airborne mercury emissions to assist in watershed planning: Office of Wetlands, Oceans, and Watersheds, accessed January 2009 at *http://www.epa.gov/owow/tmdl/techsupp.html*.

U.S. Environmental Protection Agency, 2009, Guidance for implementing the January 2001 methylmercury water quality criterion: Office of Science and Technology, EPA–823–R–09–002, accessed May 2009 at *http://www.epa.gov/waterscience/criteria/methylmercury/pdf/guidance-final.pdf*.

U.S. Fish and Wildlife Service and U.S. Census Bureau, 2003, 2001 National survey of fishing, hunting, and wildlife-associated recreation in Indiana, 86 p.

U.S. Geological Survey, 2008, National Water Information System: Web interface, surface-water data for Indiana: Accessed June 2008 at *http://waterdata.usgs.gov/in/nwis/sw/*.

Walling, D.E., 1983, The sediment delivery problem: Journal of Hydrology, v. 65, p. 209–237.

Wilde, F.D. and Gibs, Jacob, 1998, Turbidity, *in* National field manual for the collection of water-quality data: U.S. Geological Survey Techniques of Water-Resources Investigations, book 9, chap. A6.7, 30 p.

Appendix 1: Supplemental Data

Some station names in this appendix are slightly abbreviated. See table 1 in main part of report for full names.

Table 1– 1. Correlations of mercury concentrations with instantaneous streamflow at monitoring stations on Indiana streams, 2002–2006.

Station number	Station name	Correlation coefficient for mercury[1] and instantaneous streamflow at time of sample collection			
		Unfiltered total mercury	Estimated particulate total mercury	Filtered total mercury	Unfiltered methyl-mercury
1	Fall Creek near Fortville	0.95	−0.03	0.84	0.72
2	Eel River near Logansport	.89	− .08	.82	.70
3	Tippecanoe River at Winimac	.25	.33	.41	.49
4	Wildcat Creek near Lafayette	.78	− .03	.65	.36
5	Wabash River at Terre Haute	.26	− .01	.44	− .04
6	Mills Creek at Cagles Mill Dam	.16	− .08	.04	− .29
7	White River near Centerton	.78	− .19	.45	.16
8	White River at Nora	.85	.40	.87	.52
9	Sugar Creek near New Palestine	.83	− .05	.72	.31
10	East Fork Whitewater River near Brookville	.26	.16	.19	− .21
11	Vernon Fork Muscatatuck River at Vernon	.89	− .04	.82	.46
12	East Fork White River at Seymour	.84	− .10	.67	.68
13	Blue River at Fredericksburg	.20	.09	.04	.01
14	Patoka River at Winslow	.38	− .01	.46	.12
15	White River at Petersburg	.10	.52	.04	− .75
16	Busseron Creek near Carlisle	.75	− .14	.34	− .28
17	Mississinewa River near Peoria	.50	.16	.65	− .22
18	Wabash River near Huntington	.80	.01	.71	− .11
19	Maumee River at New Haven	.72	− .17	.76	.03
20	Fish Creek near Artic	.76	− .22	.93	.02
21	St. Joseph River at Elkhart	.53	.39	.64	.34
22	Trail Creek at Michigan City	.64	.18	− .06	− .02
23	Deep River at Lake George at Hobart	.83	.26	.77	.36
24	Kankakee River at Shelby	.56	.06	.70	.66
25	Wabash River at Vincennes	.34	− .29	.85	− .48
26	Wabash River at Mt. Carmel, Ill.	.99	− .46	.89	− .01

[1]Pearson correlation coefficient computed with statistical software (S-Plus, Tibco Software, 2008); censored mercury concentrations were set equal to half the reporting limit for computing correlations.

Table 1– 2.   Statistical values separating categories of daily average streamflow at monitoring stations on Indiana streams, 2002–2006.

[ft³/s, cubic feet per second; streamflow categories are low (less than or equal to the 10th percentile), medium (greater than the 10th percentile and less than or equal to the median); high (greater than the median and less than or equal to the 90th percentile); and event (greater than the 90th percentile)]

Station number	Station name	Daily average streamflow (ft³/s)[1]		
		10th percentile	Median	90th percentile
1	Fall Creek near Fortville	51	150	486
2	Eel River near Logansport	169	438	1,770
3	Tippecanoe River at Winimac	270	628	1,910
4	Wildcat Creek near Lafayette	152	469	1,920
5	Wabash River at Terre Haute	3,030	8,705	30,900
6	Mills Creek at Cagles Mill Dam	28	216	1,300
7	White River near Centerton	730	2,020	7,165
8	White River at Nora	309	905	3,624
9	Sugar Creek near New Palestine	10	60	319
10	East Fork Whitewater River near Brookville	53	265	1,305
11	Vernon Fork Muscatatuck River at Vernon	10	107	531
12	East Fork White River at Seymour	636	2,070	7,334
13	Blue River at Fredericksburg	15	197	858
14	Patoka River at Winslow	74	473	1,990
15	White River at Petersburg	3,260	10,900	29,860
16	Busseron Creek near Carlisle	11	103	667
17	Mississinewa River near Peoria	103	353	2,590
18	Wabash River near Huntington	51	280	2,370
19	Maumee River at New Haven	200	988	5,915
20	Fish Creek near Artic	10	42	228
21	St. Joseph River at Elkhart	1,230	2,485	4,990
22	Trail Creek at Michigan City	39	70	145
23	Deep River at Lake George at Hobart	16	50	316
24	Kankakee River at Shelby	629	1,290	3,160
25	Wabash River at Vincennes	3,700	9,960	31,940
26	Wabash River at Mt. Carmel, Ill.	8,662	26,800	74,300

[1] Daily average streamflow for calendar years 2002–2006 from the USGS streamflow gaging station at or near the monitoring station (U.S. Geological Survey, 2008).

Table 1-3. Annual stream loads and yields of unfiltered total mercury and unfiltered methylmercury in watersheds upstream from monitoring stations on Indiana streams, 2002–2006

[g/yr, gram per year; µg/m²/yr, microgram per square meter per year; ND, not determined]

Station[1] number	Station name	Year	Annual stream load of total mercury (g/yr)	Standard error of prediction[2] for annual stream load of total mercury (percent)	Annual stream yield of total mercury (µg/m²/yr)	Annual stream load of methylmercury (g/yr)	Standard error of prediction[2] for annual stream load of methylmercury (percent)	Annual stream yield of methylmercury (µg/m²/yr)
1	Fall Creek near Fortville	2002	5,184	35.5	11.6	ND	ND	ND
		2003	15,222	151	34.1	ND	ND	ND
		2004	5,274	32.1	11.8	ND	ND	ND
		2005	11,190	77.1	25.0	ND	ND	ND
		2006	2,723	9.7	6.1	ND	ND	ND
2	Eel River near Logansport	2002	6,384	13.7	3.1	129	4.5	0.06
		2003	5,276	2.0	2.6	135	5.5	.07
		2004	7,604	2.8	3.7	175	6.1	.09
		2005	13,399	73.4	6.6	165	21	.08
		2006	5,519	3.3	2.7	136	2.7	.07
3	Tippecanoe River at Winimac	2002	2,016	2.0	.83	101	2.1	.04
		2003	1,385	1.4	.57	63	1.4	.03
		2004	1,834	1.5	.75	85	1.6	.03
		2005	2,049	1.6	.84	98	1.7	.04
		2006	1,877	2.3	.77	101	2.5	.04
4	Wildcat Creek near Lafayette	2002	14,260	11.5	6.9	ND	ND	ND
		2003	65,549	1,710	31.9	ND	ND	ND
		2004	35,973	409	17.5	ND	ND	ND
		2005	52,220	1,040	25.4	ND	ND	ND
		2006	17,934	11.4	8.7	ND	ND	ND

Table 1–3. Annual stream loads and yields of unfiltered total mercury and unfiltered methylmercury in watersheds upstream from monitoring stations on Indiana streams, 2002–2006.—Continued

[g/yr, gram per year; μg/m²/yr, microgram per square meter per year; ND, not determined]

Station[1] number	Station name	Year	Annual stream load of total mercury (g/yr)	Standard error of prediction[2] for annual stream load of total mercury (percent)	Annual stream yield of total mercury (μg/m²/yr)	Annual stream load of methylmercury (g/yr)	Standard error of prediction[2] for annual stream load of methylmercury (percent)	Annual stream yield of methylmercury (μg/m²/yr)
5	Wabash River at Terre Haute	2002	65,418	1.4	2.0	2,100	2.5	.07
		2003	71,823	1.3	2.2	2,335	2.5	.07
		2004	66,939	1.2	2.1	2,172	2.3	.07
		2005	51,177	1.9	1.6	1,899	2.9	.06
		2006	71,267	1.0	2.2	2,186	2.1	.07
7	White River near Centerton	2002	189,458	28.7	30.0	565	143	.09
		2003	451,023	92.5	71.3	638	2,960	.10
		2004	83,911	9.6	13.3	448	14.5	.07
		2005	438,960	85.3	69.4	520	3,360	.08
		2006	87,307	5.0	13.8	674	5.4	.11
8	White River at Nora	2002	44,518	24.7	14.1	ND	ND	ND
		2003	119,475	32.3	37.9	ND	ND	ND
		2004	19,468	8.8	6.2	ND	ND	ND
		2005	121,137	40.2	38.5	ND	ND	ND
		2006	18,200	5.1	5.8	ND	ND	ND
9	Sugar Creek near New Palestine	2002	434	2.7	1.8	9.6	4.1	.04
		2003	350	2.1	1.4	14	4.3	.06
		2004	436	3.1	1.8	9.4	4.3	.04
		2005	702	3.8	2.9	14	5.3	.06
		2006	533	2.3	2.2	15	4.1	.06

Table 1-3. Annual stream loads and yields of unfiltered total mercury and unfiltered methylmercury in watersheds upstream from monitoring stations on Indiana streams, 2002–2006.—Continued

[g/yr, gram per year; µg/m²/yr, microgram per square meter per year; ND, not determined]

Station[1] number	Station name	Year	Annual stream load of total mercury (g/yr)	Standard error of prediction[2] for annual stream load of total mercury (percent)	Annual stream yield of total mercury (µg/m²/yr)	Annual stream load of methylmercury (g/yr)	Standard error of prediction[2] for annual stream load of methylmercury (percent)	Annual stream yield of methylmercury (µg/m²/yr)
11	Vernon Fork Muscatatuck River at Vernon	2002	7,897	6.2	15.4	52	1.8	.10
		2003	6,459	9.7	12.6	36	1.9	.07
		2004	4,708	5.6	9.2	32	1.5	.06
		2005	5,757	7.8	11.2	23	1.4	.04
		2006	8,649	8.3	16.9	77	6.6	.15
12	East Fork White River at Seymour	2002	325,707	77.6	53.8	ND	ND	ND
		2003	70,649	9.0	11.7	ND	ND	ND
		2004	203,790	234	33.6	ND	ND	ND
		2005	477,625	322	78.9	ND	ND	ND
		2006	290,694	65.2	48.0	ND	ND	ND
13	Blue River at Fredericksburg	2002	759	2.0	1.0	27	3.7	.04
		2003	639	1.7	.87	24	3.2	.03
		2004	923	2.4	1.3	31	4.1	.04
		2005	566	2.2	.77	20	3.7	.03
		2006	930	2.0	1.3	32	3.7	.04
14	Patoka River at Winslow	2002	13,558	2.0	8.7	158	4.0	.10
		2003	7,588	1.5	4.9	113	2.7	.07
		2004	8,513	1.6	5.5	124	2.8	.08
		2005	8,056	2.0	5.2	97	3.8	.06
		2006	ND	ND	ND	ND	ND	ND

Table 1–3. Annual stream loads and yields of unfiltered total mercury and unfiltered methylmercury in watersheds upstream from monitoring stations on Indiana streams, 2002–2006.—Continued

[g/yr, gram per year; µg/m²/yr, microgram per square meter per year; ND, not determined]

Station[1] number	Station name	Year	Annual stream load of total mercury (g/yr)	Standard error of prediction[2] for annual stream load of total mercury (percent)	Annual stream yield of total mercury (µg/m²/yr)	Annual stream load of methylmercury (g/yr)	Standard error of prediction[2] for annual stream load of methylmercury (percent)	Annual stream yield of methylmercury (µg/m²/yr)
16	Busseron Creek near Carlisle	2002	3,408	14.6	5.8	76	.9	.13
		2003	2,049	5.4	3.5	68	.7	.11
		2004	1,329	24.9	2.2	45	.7	.08
		2005	3,354	78.1	5.7	72	1.0	.12
		2006	3,759	12.4	6.4	105	.8	.18
19	Maumee River at New Haven	2002	20,841	1.4	4.1	330	2.2	.07
		2003	38,085	1.5	7.5	554	3.0	.11
		2004	23,855	1.3	4.7	376	2.3	.07
		2005	27,399	1.5	5.4	398	3.5	.08
		2006	27,367	1.2	5.4	437	1.9	.09
20	Fish Creek near Artic	2002	402	1.9	1.6	ND	ND	ND
		2003	324	1.6	1.3	ND	ND	ND
		2004	290	1.6	1.2	ND	ND	ND
		2005	396	1.9	1.6	ND	ND	ND
		2006	446	1.6	1.8	ND	ND	ND
21	St. Joseph River at Elkhart	2002	7,314	1.8	.84	ND	ND	ND
		2003	4,141	1.3	.47	ND	ND	ND
		2004	6,848	1.6	.78	ND	ND	ND
		2005	6,693	1.9	.76	ND	ND	ND
		2006	6,774	1.5	.77	ND	ND	ND

Table 1–3. Annual stream loads and yields of unfiltered total mercury and unfiltered methylmercury in watersheds upstream from monitoring stations on Indiana streams, 2002–2006.—Continued

[g/yr, gram per year; µg/m²/yr, microgram per square meter per year; ND, not determined]

Station[1] number	Station name	Year	Annual stream load of total mercury (g/yr)	Standard error of prediction[2] for annual stream load of total mercury (percent)	Annual stream yield of total mercury (µg/m²/yr)	Annual stream load of methylmercury (g/yr)	Standard error of prediction[2] for annual stream load of methylmercury (percent)	Annual stream yield of methylmercury (µg/m²/yr)
23	Deep River at Lake George at Hobart	2002	451	1.4	1.4	9.0	2.1	.03
		2003	408	1.2	1.3	8.7	1.9	.03
		2004	462	1.1	1.4	10	1.8	.03
		2005	460	1.3	1.4	9.2	2.1	.03
		2006	736	1.2	2.3	15	2.0	.05
24	Kankakee River at Shelby	2002	7,190	1.7	1.6	ND	ND	ND
		2003	4,439	1.3	1.0	ND	ND	ND
		2004	5,684	1.3	1.2	ND	ND	ND
		2005	6,960	1.7	1.5	ND	ND	ND
		2006	5,813	1.3	1.3	ND	ND	ND

[1]Stream loads and stream yields for total mercury and methylmercury were not calculated for stations 6, 10, 15, 17, 18, 22, 25, and 26 because of insufficient data.

[2]The Standard Error of Prediction (SEP) begins with an estimate of parameter uncertainty (the Standard Error) and adds the unexplained variability about the model (random error). Because SEP incorporates parameter uncertainty and random error, it is larger than the Standard Error and provides a better description of how closely estimated loads correspond to actual loads. The SEP is the preferred method of describing uncertainty in loads (Runkel and others, 2004). Here, the SEP is presented as a percentage of the annual load.

Table 1–4. Model characteristics of annual stream loads of mercury in watersheds upstream from monitoring stations on Indiana streams, 2002–2006.

[UTHG, unfiltered total mercury; UMHG, unfiltered methylmercury; —, insufficient data; $\ln Q = \ln(\text{streamflow}) - \text{center of } \ln(\text{streamflow})$]

Station number[1]	Station name	Number of samples with UTHG for regression model	Average standard error of prediction for stream load[2] of UTHG (percent)	Number of samples with UMHG for regression model	Average standard error of prediction for stream load[2] of UMHG (percent)	Predefined load model[3] selected by software for equation: ln (instantaneous stream mercury load) =
1	Fall Creek near Fortville	18	89.3	—	—	$a0 + a1 \ln Q + a2 \ln Q^2$
2	Eel River near Logansport	18	29.4	10	8.40	$a0 + a1 \ln Q + a2 \ln Q^2$
3	Tippecanoe River at Winimac	18	1.80	8	1.91	$a0 + a1 \ln Q$
4	Wildcat Creek near Lafayette	17	974	—	—	$a0 + a1 \ln Q + a2 \ln Q^2$
5	Wabash River at Terre Haute	18	1.36	14	2.46	$a0 + a1 \ln Q + a2 \ln Q^2$
7	White River near Centerton	18	68.7	15	1,310	$a0 + a1 \ln Q + a2 \ln Q^2$
8	White River at Nora	18	31.3	—	—	$a0 + a1 \ln Q + a2 \ln Q^2$
9	Sugar Creek near New Palestine	17	2.91	8	4.45	$a0 + a1 \ln Q$
11	Vernon Fork Muscatatuck River at Vernon	17	7.60	14	1.69	$a0 + a1 \ln Q + a2 \ln Q^2$
12	East Fork White River at Seymour	17	180	—	—	$a0 + a1 \ln Q + a2 \ln Q^2$
13	Blue River at Fredericksburg	17	2.07	8	3.72	$a0 + a1 \ln Q$
14	Patoka River at Winslow	17	1.79	13	3.36	$a0 + a1 \ln Q$
16	Busseron Creek near Carlisle	17	29.0	11	.85	$a0 + a1 \ln Q + a2 \ln Q^2$
19	Maumee River at New Haven	16	7.54	13	2.60	$a0 + a1 \ln Q$
20	Fish Creek near Artic	15	2.60	—	—	$a0 + a1 \ln Q$
21	St. Joseph River at Elkhart	16	1.19	—	—	$a0 + a1 \ln Q$
23	Deep River at Lake George at Hobart	16	1.26	9	1.99	$a0 + a1 \ln Q$
24	Kankakee River at Shelby	15	1.49	—	—	$a0 + a1 \ln Q$

[1] Stream loads and stream yields for total mercury and methylmercury were not calculated for stations 6, 10, 15, 17, 18, 22, 25, and 26 because of insufficient data.

[2] Average standard error of prediction for stream load of mercury is the average of the annual standard error of prediction values divided by the average annual stream load of mercury, expressed as a percentage.

[3] Models from Runkel and others (2004).

Table 1–5. Number of stationary sources of mercury emissions to the atmosphere and annual mercury emissions in 2002 and 2005 for watersheds upstream from monitoring stations on Indiana streams.

[kg, kilogram]

Station number	Station name for upstream watershed	2002		2005	
		Number of stationary sources of mercury emissions	Annual mercury emissions (kg)	Number of stationary sources of mercury emissions	Annual mercury emissions (kg)
1	Fall Creek near Fortville	1	0.04	0	0
2	Eel River near Logansport	2	208	2	81.9
3	Tippecanoe River at Winimac	5	28.3	4	31.5
4	Wildcat Creek near Lafayette	6	10.3	6	1.49
5	Wabash River at Terre Haute	25	1,097	22	376
6	Mills Creek at Cagles Mill Dam	0	0	0	0
7	White River near Centerton	20	152	13	189
8	White River at Nora	4	5.7	4	7.74
9	Sugar Creek near New Palestine	0	0	0	0
10	East Fork Whitewater River near Brookville	1	17.4	2	11.3
11	Vernon Fork Muscatatuck River at Vernon	0	0	0	0
12	East Fork White River at Seymour	8	25.8	5	32.2
13	Blue River at Fredericksburg	0	0	0	0
14	Patoka River at Winslow	4	7.63	2	.73
15	White River at Petersburg	20	617	18	586
16	Busseron Creek near Carlisle	0	0	0	0
17	Mississinewa River near Peoria	3	2.44	0	0
18	Wabash River near Huntington	1	1.47	0	0
19	Maumee River at New Haven	7	339	5	250
20	Fish Creek near Artic	0	0	0	0
21	St. Joseph River at Elkhart	5	15.3	2	6.41
22	Trail Creek at Michigan City	2	59.8	2	61.3
23	Deep River at Lake George at Hobart	0	0	0	0
24	Kankakee River at Shelby	8	187	7	197
25	Wabash River at Vincennes	5	55.9	4	73.6
26	Wabash River at Mt. Carmel, Ill.	1	.05	1	.06

Table 1–6. Percentages of land-cover classes in watersheds upstream from monitoring stations on Indiana streams.

[Percentages computed as land are in watershed in each land-cover class divided by the total watershed upstream drainage area, multiplied by 100; —, no area in land-cover class; <, less than]

Land cover class[1]	Monitoring station number for upstream watershed												
	1	2	3	4	5	6	7	8	9	10	11	12	13
Low intensity residential	4.15	0.61	0.92	2.21	1.02	0.54	8.31	4.50	1.55	1.84	0.74	1.85	0.84
High intensity residential	.22	.06	.14	.21	.27	.03	1.07	.49	.05	.48	.05	.20	.06
Commercial/industrial/transportation	.87	.25	.48	.87	.56	.23	3.19	1.45	.35	1.23	.30	.84	.16
Bare rock/sand/clay	—	—	—	—	.01	—	—	—	—	—	—	—	—
Quarries/strip mines/gravel pits	.11	—	< .01	< .01	.05	.07	.06	.07	—	—	.03	.01	.06
Coal mine lands[2]	—	—	—	—	.32	—	—	—	—	—	—	—	—
Transitional	—	< .01	—	< .01	.01	.16	.05	—	—	—	.31	.05	—
Deciduous forest	5.45	8.25	8.79	3.09	8.17	15.20	6.23	4.05	4.96	17.03	33.02	8.66	24.66
Evergreen forest	< .01	.03	.12	.01	.29	.11	.03	.02	.01	.28	1.20	.08	2.77
Mixed forest	< .01	< .01	.01	< .01	.17	< .01	.01	< .01	< .01	.05	.10	.01	.18
Shrubland	—	—	—	—	.01	—	—	—	—	—	—	—	—
Grassland/herbaceous	—	< .01	.01	—	.39	—	—	—	—	—	—	—	—
Orchards/vineyards/other	—	—	—	—	.02	.02	.02	—	—	.03	—	.01	—
Pasture/hay	19.54	15.73	1.66	1.66	1.53	18.28	16.67	13.27	16.44	16.37	38.94	2.09	4.42
Rowcrop	66.43	72.81	72.80	8.24	75.29	64.00	6.16	72.26	75.45	59.57	24.33	66.45	3.51
Small grains	—	—	—	—	.01	—	—	—	—	—	—	—	—
Fallow	2.20	.03	.14	1.18	.45	.15	2.47	2.01	.23	.30	.12	.59	.06
Woody wetlands	.75	1.37	3.02	1.12	1.48	.11	.75	1.09	.69	.61	.42	.74	.07
Emergent herbaceous wetlands	.12	.26	.83	.07	.22	.01	.05	.06	.03	.03	.01	.02	.01
Open water	.17	.59	2.09	.34	.81	1.06	.94	.72	.23	2.18	.44	.39	—

Table 1–6.   Percentages of land-cover classes in watersheds upstream from monitoring stations on Indiana streams. —Continued

[Percentages computed as land are in watershed in each land-cover class divided by the total watershed upstream drainage area, multiplied by 100; —, no area in land-cover class; <, less than]

Land cover class[1]	Monitoring station number for upstream watershed												
	14	15	16	17	18	19	20	21	22	23	24	25	26
Low intensity residential	.66	2.80	1.35	2.04	.76	2.54	.38	1.31	6.24	8.70	1.06	1.02	1.65
High intensity residential	.09	.33	.16	.24	.14	.47	.06	.15	3.40	6.40	.29	.28	.29
Commercial/industrial/transportation	.26	1.09	.60	.63	.41	1.16	.19	.64	3.69	3.57	.58	.58	.76
Bare rock/sand/clay	—	<.01	<.01	—	—	—	—	—	.08	<.01	.03	.01	.01
Quarries/strip mines/gravel pits	.24	.12	1.70	.04	.06	.02	—	.01	—	<.01	.03	.08	.10
Coal mine lands[2]	5.38	1.27	19.61	—	—	—	—	—	—	—	—	.79	1.24
Transitional	.31	.25	.21	—	.02	.02	.11	.03	—	—	.01	.01	.12
Deciduous forest	37.15	23.21	2.36	7.32	5.55	9.84	17.82	14.64	27.07	14.29	9.34	9.05	15.39
Evergreen forest	2.09	.66	1.18	.04	.05	.10	.15	.32	9.00	3.31	1.70	.33	.54
Mixed forest	.06	.04	3.42	.01	.01	.03	.11	.03	2.35	—	.17	.29	.18
Shrubland	—	—	.49	—	—	—	—	—	—	.51	—	.02	.01
Grassland/herbaceous	—	.00	4.63	—	—	.04	.44	.01	6.21	4.16	2.08	.48	.28
Orchards/vineyards/other	—	.01	.03	—	—	—	—	.04	—	—	.03	.02	.02
Pasture/hay	24.08	21.01	11.22	11.64	9.35	16.23	29.61	16.19	14.63	14.48	11.91	11.84	16.92
Rowcrop	26.72	47.16	31.81	75.47	79.88	66.54	45.41	57.45	16.94	33.79	68.22	71.87	59.57
Small grains	<.01	.08	—	—	—	—	—	—	.12	.08	.04	.03	.04
Fallow	.06	.75	1.08	.66	.10	.32	—	.34	1.66	5.61	.38	.49	.58
Woody wetlands	.64	.68	5.94	.99	.62	1.71	2.97	4.91	6.36	2.60	2.28	1.74	1.42
Emergent herbaceous wetlands	.11	.04	.40	.09	.12	.25	.70	1.11	1.37	1.16	.77	.23	.15
Open water	2.70	.95	2.20	.84	2.92	.74	2.04	2.82	.89	1.34	1.04	.94	.96

[1]Land-cover class description from National Land-Cover Dataset (Multi-Resolution Land Characteristics Consortium, 1992).

[2]Coal mine lands supplemental data for active and abandoned (reclaimed/unreclaimed) aboveground coal mines (Eaton, 2002 and Indiana Geological Survey, 2002)